Japan Economic/Demographic Information

Geographic area:	145,856 sq. miles
Topography:	Four main islands—Honshu (mainland), Hokkaido, Kyushu and Shikoku
Government type:	Parliamentary democracy
Capital:	Tokyo
Population:	123,231,000
Population density:	844 per sq. mile, 76.7% urban
Agricultural products:	Rice, vegetables, fruits and sugar
Industrial products:	Metals, chemicals, textiles and electronics
Natural resources:	Fish, oil, natural gas, negligible amount of mineral resources
Literacy:	99%
Defense:	Less than 1% GNP
National budget:	$470 billion
Balance of payments:	+ $85 billion
Inflation:	0.7%
Gross National Product:	$2.1 trillion
Gross Domestic Product:	$1.6 trillion
International reserves: (less gold)	$98 billion
Gold reserves:	24.2 million fine troy ounces
Major imports:	Fuels, machinery, manufactured goods, raw materials and foodstuffs
Imports:	$187 billion
U.S.	20%
Middle East	26%
Southeast Asia	22%
European Community	6%
Major Exports:	Machinery, electrical equipment, motor vehicles, chemicals and manufactured goods
Exports:	$264 billion
U.S.	37%
Southeast Asia	23%
European Community	12%
Labor Profile:	
Agriculture, Forestry, Fishing	8.8%
Manufacturing	25.02%
Transport./Communications	5.91%
Construction	9.13%
Other	51.17%

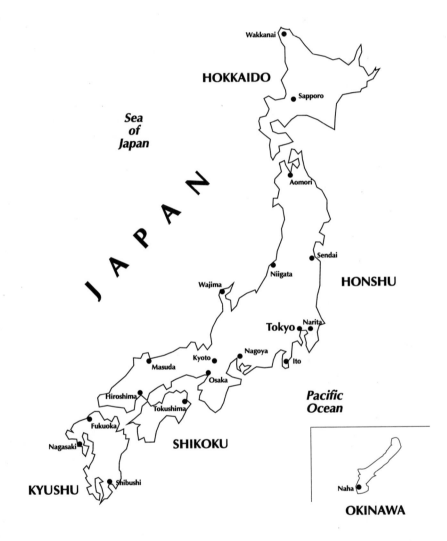

Wakkanai

HOKKAIDO

Sapporo

Sea
of
Japan

Aomori

J A P A N

Sendai

Niigata

Wajima

HONSHU

Tokyo Narita

Nagoya

Kyoto

Ito

Masuda

Osaka

Pacific
Ocean

Hiroshima

Tokushima

Fukuoka

SHIKOKU

Nagasaki

Naha

Shibushi

KYUSHU

OKINAWA

UNLOCKING JAPAN'S MARKETS

SEIZING MARKETING AND DISTRIBUTION OPPORTUNITIES IN TODAY'S JAPAN

MICHAEL R. CZINKOTA

JON WORONOFF

FOREWORD BY C. WILLIAM VERITY,
FORMER U.S. SECRETARY OF COMMERCE

AMERICAN
MARKETING
ASSOCIATION

PROBUS PUBLISHING COMPANY
Chicago, Illinois

This publication is designed to provide accurate and authoritative information in regard to the subject matter covered. It is sold with the understanding that the publisher is not engaged in rendering legal, accounting or other professional service.

Library of Congress Cataloging in Publication Data Available

ISBN 1-55738-213-1

Printed in the United States of America

KP

1 2 3 4 5 6 7 8 9 0

To Ilona, my csillag and gardener. MRC

ఎ&

To Simon and Tami, JW

OTHER JAPAN TITLES
FROM PROBUS

Japan Inc.: Global Strategies of Japanese Trading Corporations, Max Eli

The Pacific Rim Futures and Options Markets: A Comprehensive, Country-by-Country Reference to the World's Fastest-Growing Financial Markets, Keith K.H. Park & Steven A. Schoenfeld

The Japanese Bond Markets: An Overview & Analysis, ed. Frank J. Fabozzi

CSFB Guide to the Yen Bond Markets

FORTHCOMING JAPAN TITLES
FROM PROBUS

Invest Japan: The Structure, Performance and Opportunities of Japan's Stock, Bond and Fund Markets, William T. Ziemba & Sandra L. Schwartz (Fall 1991)

Power Japan: How and Why the Japanese Economy Works, William T. Ziemba & Sandra L. Schwartz (Fall 1991)

Venture Japan: How Growing Companies Worldwide Can Tap into the Japanese Venture Capital Markets, James W. Borton (Fall 1991)

Contents

Foreword, by C. William Verity   vii
Acknowledgements   xi

1. Why Japan? And How?   1

Part I
Open . . . Part Way
2. A Rather Special Market   9
3. Impediments, Ordinary   13
4. Getting in Step   19
5. Impediments, Extraordinary   25

Part II
Corporate Connections
6. The Inescapable Groupings   31
7. The Big Eight . . . And More   39
8. Enterprise Groupings   47
9. From Manufacturing to Marketing   57
10. Living with the System   65

Part III
The Distribution Maze
11. Distribution as a Market Factor   75
12. A Brief Historical Review   81
13. The Wholesale Sector   87
14. The Retail Sector   99

Part IV
Changes in the Distribution System
15. Changes in Wholesale Structure and Institutions   111
16. Changes in Retail Structure and Institutions   117
17. Changes in Consumer Behavior   131
18. The Role of Distribution Information and Technology   135

Part V
Entering the Market
19. Alternative Routes   141
20. Exporting, Licensing and Franchising   147
21. Joint Ventures   155
22. Wholly-Owned Ventures   161
23. Acquisitions   167

Part VI
Mutual Adjustments
24. Doing Like the Japanese   173
25. Coming Closer Together   183

Glossary   191
Acronyms   193
Bibliography   195
Index   207

Foreword

C. William Verity

I was most fortunate to have Michael Czinkota as a Deputy Assistant Secretary for International Trade when I served President Reagan as Secretary of Commerce. And the reader of this splendid treatise on *Unlocking Japan's Market* is most fortunate to have such a knowledgeable guide to learning how to trade successfully in the world's second largest market—Japan.

My first official international assignment from President Reagan occurred early in my tenure as Secretary of Commerce. Prime Minister Nakasone had been replaced by Prime Minister Takeshita with a new cabinet. Our trade relations with Japan were deteriorating. Congress was bashing the Japanese as they worked over the Omnibus Trade Bill of 1987, and the President wanted to improve our relationship with the new government of Japan.

I was delighted with the opportunity. While at Armco Steel Corp., I had done business with Japanese steel companies for 25 years. Armco licensed technology to Nippon Steel Co., and we engaged in joint research efforts. Mr. Toyota dropped by to see me in Washington to thank me once more for helping Toyota receive deep drawing steel sheets from Nippon Steel. He said it gave Toyota the edge in supplying Japanese autos with the finest deep drawing cold rolled steel. I had many friends in the business community in Tokyo. And I had another big advantage. My father had been "industrial advisor" to General MacArthur from 1948–50. He had persuaded the General not to ship Japan's largest steel plant to the Philippines, but instead rebuild it so it could help in rebuilding the infrastructure of the Japanese industrial system. As a result, the Japanese considered the Veritys as friends.

At this particular time, the United States was having difficulty with Japan because the Japanese would not open their construction market to U.S. contractors. The Kansai Airport was the prime example. The Japanese would also not open their market to imported beef and orange juice. And though the Japanese had agreed to a patent secrecy agreement over 35 years ago, they would never sign the agreement and therefore continued to violate American patent laws. This very first trip as Secretary taught me how difficult it was to move the Japanese towards freer trade. In fact, I spent the rest of my tenure as Secretary in trying to improve our trade relationships and to create a constructive dialogue based on mutual responsibilities and shared leadership.

This was a lofty goal. The facts were that the Congress was about to pass an omnibus trade bill that frightened the Japanese, and the trade deficit between our two countries remained obscenely high. The Minister of Trade and Industry (MITI), Tamura, was convinced that America's trading problems with Japan were caused by poor quality and high-priced products rather than the convoluted Japanese distribution system, which, fundamentally, blocked many foreign products from reaching the Japanese consumer. The Japanese were prepared to play hardball with us on trade, but they desired a resolution of the problems between us, many of which resulted from the Japanese customs and traditions. I came to believe that it would be essential for the United States to go on the offensive if we were to improve our trade with Japan. A good example was our special project "Mission Japan—With America's Best."

In some of the many discussions between Minister Tamura and myself, he agreed to a "trial run" to find out whether the U.S. could produce quality products at a competitive price—or whether the problem was the Japanese distribution system.

He selected five product categories: Sporting and leisure goods, jewelry, furniture and processed foods. He suggested that we find five companies in each category that were interested in doing business in Japan, and that he would circumvent the normal distribution system by allowing these products to go directly to the consumer outlet (store).

In September of 1988, we (the Department of Commerce) flew the CEOs of 25 companies to Japan. All of these 25 companies produced high quality products and all were interested in the Japanese market—and committed to staying in it to service their products.

Minister Tamura lived up to his agreement. Each company had a special agent from MITI who mothered that company's product through the distribution channels—and directly on to the shelves of the department store.

It was an eye-opener for all of us.

The U.S. quality was as good—or better.

The U.S. products were cheaper than the Japanese products. One of the 25, Winnebago, sold many of their fully equipped campers, even though there are few camping sites in Japan. They were used as an addition to present homes. They provided an extra kitchen, shower stall, refrigerator, bedroom, etc.

Michael Czinkota was there—in the middle of all the discussions and planning and negotiations.

Michael had for many years been a student of the Japanese market. He had lectured on the subject. And now as a Deputy Assistant Secretary for International Trade, he immersed himself in the subject. Mission Japan was one of his finest hours. I believe the integrative approach in this book is possible only because of his stint at Commerce, and his extensive background in business, policy, and academe.

For anyone who wants to deal with Japan in a knowledgeable, constructive way, I believe reading this book would be extremely worthwhile. The book goes beyond covering the Japan issue simply from an academic, policy or business perspective. Rather, it tries to integrate all three of them by offering realistic insights into what makes the Japanese market work, and it provides suggestions to foreign companies on how to operate within the system.

This very thoughtful book focuses attention on the Japanese business structure, and in particular the distribution system. It explains knowledgeably the "keiretsu," which provide strong linkages among Japanese firms. It incorporates detailed examinations of the distribution system which has proven so often to be the formidable barrier to market penetration. It highlights distribution changes which offer opportunities to foreign firms to be successful in Japan.

The book does not engage in Japan-bashing. It acknowledges the importance of the Japanese market and places the trade relationship in the context of the global aspirations for both the United States and Japan. It urges a policy of mutual adjustment and collaboration, because we are faced with problems too large and too important to be addressed by one nation alone.

The book describes why Japan is a very special market and why it is necessary to get in step with the way they do business. It describes the impediments to doing business with Japan that are the usual kind, and the very unusual. It describes the tight relationship between the large Japanese corporations and their manufacturing to marketing systems.

Where the book truly excels is in describing the Distribution Maze. It explores the wholesale sectors and the retail sectors and their relationships. It then describes the changes in the structure and institutions in wholesale and retail, and outlines graphically the changes in consumer behavior—and how rapidly this change has occurred. And lastly, it describes how to enter the market, the value of joint ventures, wholly-owned ventures, and acquisitions.

The book ends up with a fascinating chapter on mutual adjustments, which describes how we can do it like the Japanese and how we can come closer together by better understanding the methods used by the Japanese in capturing markets throughout the world.

If you are thinking of doing business with Japan, then I highly recommend that you read *Unlocking Japan's Markets*. If you are not thinking of doing business with Japan, then I would urge you to reconsider, because trading opportunities in Japan will remain positive for many years to come. And those who develop a relationship the soonest will be the beneficiaries of this large and profitable trading relationship.

C. William Verity

Acknowledgements

In writing a book, one communicates accumulated experience, reflections and thoughts. None of these happen in a vacuum, but rather, are the result of interactions with people, participation in negotiations, and learning through the writings of others. This book offers only another stepping stone in the thinking about doing business in Japan, set in the foundation of many precursors.

We are grateful to many people for their help, insights and support. In particular they are Malcolm Baldrige and C. William Verity, Secretaries of Commerce, and Clayton Yeutter and William Brock, U.S. Trade Representatives, who offered the opportunity for policy involvement and insight. Very helpful were also the comments and actions by Paul Freedenberg, Takeshi Isayama, William Morris, H.P. Goldfield and Peter Pierce. On the academic side, Bernard LaLonde was a valuable ally and friend, as were Robert Green, S. Tamer Cavusgil, Ilkka Ronkainen, Douglas McCabe and Takeshi Suzuki. Many individuals in the corporate world were of major assistance, in particular Joseph Lynch of ADI, William Casselman of Popham, Haik, Lew Cramer of U.S. WEST and Raymond Waldman of Boeing. We also thank Dodwell Marketing Consultants in Tokyo, who kindly granted us permission to reprint materials from their publications.

Any errors of omission or commission are, of course, the sole responsibility of the authors.

CHAPTER

1

Why Japan? And How?

When managers plan a worldwide strategy, there is one market they cannot avoid considering—Japan. And when trade negotiators focus on markets that are crucial to maintaining a healthy trade balance, there is one they cannot forget, the very same one—Japan. There are plenty of reasons for this.

First of all, Japan is the world's second largest market after the United States. With a population of over 120 million affluent consumers, it is already more than half the size of the American market. In fact, according to 1989 statistics, it has a total gross national product of $2.8 trillion, compared to $5.2 trillion for the United States. Although the Japanese save money more, they also spend freely, so disposable income remains high.

What is more important is that, with strong economic growth and a constantly strengthening yen, this market is expanding faster than the American market and most European markets. Any company that gets in can benefit from continued expansion, as opposed to making do with a stagnant or contracting market elsewhere. According to virtually all estimates, the Japanese economy should remain buoyant and the yen should appreciate further in coming years and decades.

Aside from that, Japan offers an excellent site for industrial production, especially of sophisticated manufactured goods because of its well-trained and diligent labor force. Admittedly, labor costs are high, as are land and other expenses. But this may be justified once sales rise to a level where local production is necessary either to meet the rising demand or adapt to local requirements and tight deadlines. For the most advanced sectors, Japan is also a promising location for research and development.

So much for the carrots. They only explain why it is desirable to do business with or in Japan. But they almost pale when compared to the stick.

Japanese companies are among the world's most inventive and aggressive. They are constantly coming up with new products or improvements on old ones. And they export them with a vengeance. A foreign company that does not pay adequate attention will know what those products are, and be able to come up with equivalent or superior ones, only when it is too late. That is, after the Japanese have entered the company's domestic market and are eating away at sales. With an establishment in Japan, it is possible to know what the competition is doing much earlier, to prepare for it back home, and possibly to react first on the Japanese market.

This rationale for taking the first step was clearly stated by Abegglen and Stalk.

> Competition from the *kaisha* (Japanese corporation) can best be met, and in many cases can only be met, by market competition *inside* Japan. All too often, by the time Japanese products begin to appear in volume in Western markets, the competitive advantage has already shifted away from the Western competitor. The strategic battleground is the Japanese economy . . .[1]

It was expressed even more forcefully by Peter Grace, chairman of W.R. Grace & Co. "If we can compete with Japanese companies in Japan, we can compete with them around the world."[2]

This will explain why so many foreign companies have already entered the Japanese market one way or the other. They export to Japan, they market their own goods in Japan, they produce some of them locally, they have offices, warehouses, factories, even R&D labs. Indeed, the list of foreign companies with operations in Japan reads like a "who's who" of major multinationals with many smaller entities thrown in. Even a casual walk around Tokyo or a glance at the ads will reveal names like Coca Cola, McDonalds, IBM, BMW, Gucci, Nescafe, and so on. So it looks as if things are running quite nicely.

This impression is reinforced by articles in local dailies or special publications designed for foreign visitors.[3] They never cease playing up the "success" of one foreign company or another. They stress the large number, the size, and the profitability. Among other things, it is announced annually that foreign firms made bigger profits on the whole than Japanese firms.

But it would be unwise to give too much credence to these stories. All too many of them are inspired by the Japanese authorities. Under pressure to open the market further and make it easier for foreign companies to enter, they find it advantageous to emphasize just how many are already there and how well they are doing. In this exercise, they have no trouble locating foreign businessmen to interview and who will tell in glowing terms about their singular achievements in Japan and just how easy it is to do business there. This is good publicity for them, just as it is good public relations for the Japanese.

Just how well foreign companies are actually doing is hard to tell. Some are a definite success. They have been increasing sales and expanding operations for years. They have efficient and productive facilities that provide goods that clearly meet Japanese needs. They have a capable local staff. And they report good earnings. But others have encountered greater difficulties, and quite a few have simply had to withdraw in failure. What is no less significant is that, despite vigorous efforts, many foreign companies, including major multinationals, never managed to take root. That explains why, according to the Royal Institute of International Studies, foreigners only hold one percent of Japanese corporate assets as compared to five percent in the United States and 10 percent in Great Britain and Germany.[4] If Japan were such a receptive market, the figure would be much higher.

Open, But Not Fully

You may also read, in the same media, inspired by the same sources, and with interviews of the same foreigners, that the difficulties of doing business in Japan have already been overcome. The market is now open, it is claimed. Tariffs and quotas are less than abroad, foreigners can invest freely, buy land, acquire local companies, do business much as at home with few rules or regulations to hinder them. Foreign exports are up, they add. So there is no reason to hesitate.

Alas, this sort of comment has been made for years already, after each round of trade talks, after each market-opening package. Yet, there always seem to be new barriers, and a need for new rounds of trade talks, and then more market-opening packages. So it is clear that, while there has been change, much remains to be done. And that is why not only foreign businessmen but also foreign governments and trade negotiators cannot avoid dealing with Japan.

To give credit where credit is due, the Japanese market does not even faintly resemble the market of 20, 10, or even five years ago. Things can be done now that would have been impossible then. The climate is considerably more relaxed, government officials are more cooperative, and the public is more receptive to foreign products. These advances were not always made voluntarily, but they were made, and the Japanese should be thanked. Moreover, each time a sector was actually opened, possibilities blossomed for foreign companies, which cashed in, whether for cigarettes, alcoholic beverages, or automobiles of late.

What has not changed that much, although there has been some movement, is the distribution sector, where the number of wholesalers and retailers (and related complexity and costs) are far greater than abroad. Nor have the intercompany relations, which tend to exclude outsiders. These are the principal remaining hurdles, and, as such, they must be considered more exhaustively further on. At this point, however, it is interesting to hear the opinion not of an academic or trade negotiator but a businessman whose job it is to sell to Japan. These comments are from Edmund J. Reilly, president of Digital Equipment Corporation, Japan.

> I think people don't realize the change that has gone on in Japan. When I look back at the '70s, and in most industries, certainly within the computer industry, it was a relatively closed market. In the computer industry at that time, the duty rate was around 15 to 20% on most products, there was a quota system in place, you were not allowed to sell to the government, you were not allowed to sell to large corporations. In the '80s, all that has changed. The market is opening. All of the real substantive trading barriers have disappeared.

But, he added, "there are still barriers that relate to structural areas that are very difficult to bring down." In elucidating, he added:

> I think that simply stated, it's a lot more difficult for an American company to do business in Japan than it is for a Japanese company to do business in America. A lot of it relates to culture . . . That's the structural thing that's so difficult. The answer to that is really time. As long as these realities exist, the trade barrier will never really come down. That's a problem, today. It's hard for the governments to sit down and discuss that sort of thing; it's not tangible.[5]

So, anyone who wants to do business in Japan, or has to anyway, would be wise to ignore any claims of an open market, ready access, and potentially rich rewards. Japan is a tough market to get into; it is not easy doing business there, and the rewards will only materialize for those who do the right things. This does not make it any less important to go there. It just means that it is necessary to plan ahead more carefully, operate more intelligently, and perhaps wait a bit longer to achieve any goals than elsewhere.

That is why this book has not played down the difficulties. Indeed, if anything, it states them very clearly and shows what the traps and pitfalls are. It lets the foreign businessmen (and trade negotiators) know just what they are up against. And it indicates various ways of getting around some of the difficulties, avoiding traps and pitfalls, and adjusting to a rather different and often confusing business context.

This is not done with catch-phrases and formulas, with a short list of dos and don'ts, or the like. They can be more misleading than otherwise. Every company is different. So every company has to adopt a different approach depending on its size, product range, financial backing, and so forth. It is best, therefore, to know the possible alternatives and then pick the most appropriate ones.

In this book, we start with a description of the various barriers, from more traditional tariffs and quotas to the non-tariff barriers of today. Particular stress is placed on the distribution sector, where the biggest, most pervasive and decisive problems lie at present. This includes a survey of intercompany relations through *keiretsu* and other groupings. Then comes a thorough look at distribution, wholesaling and retailing, including impending changes. Later sections show the various ways of getting into the distribution network, tying up with Japanese firms or going it alone. Whatever the choice, every foreign company must learn to do business in Japan and adjust its corporate culture thereto. Finally, there is a look toward the future, since trade in general and distribution in particular are in flux.

Notes

1. James C. Abegglen and George Stalk Jr., *Kaisha, The Japanese Corporation* (New York: Basic Books, 1985), p. 214.

2. *Focus Japan*, January 1990, p. 8.

3. Examples are *Focus Japan, JETRO Monitor, Look Japan, Tradepia,* and others.

4. *The Wall Street Journal*, April 9, 1990.

5. *Look Japan*, December 1989, p. 13.

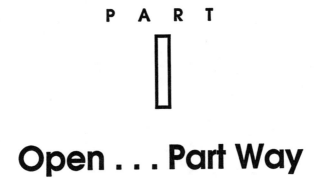

PART

Open . . . Part Way

C H A P T E R

2

A Rather Special Market

International commerce should, or so the theory goes, contribute to international understanding and mutual prosperity. Yet, at least as concerns the relations between Japan and its partners, the result has been steadily growing friction and endless rounds of recrimination about who is getting the most out of trade.

Trade conflicts have existed in one form or another for over three decades. Initially, the tension was limited to specific sectors where Japan sold too much and hurt domestic industries. It has since spread and become more general as Japan's trade surpluses grew. From concern with Japanese exports, the focus shifted increasingly to annoyance at not being able to coax Japan into importing more. The situation was already unpleasant during the 1960s and 1970s when trade was still expanding nicely; it has become more painful in a time of relative stagnation.

In a world economy where it is hard to make both ends meet, it is irritating to find that one country has been doing so well. Aside from two brief periods after the first and second oil crises in 1973 and 1979, Japan has run a positive trade balance. Indeed, the balance almost exploded in recent years, starting with a modest $5 billion surplus in 1981.[1] By fiscal 1983, it had reached a record high of $23 billion, which was dwarfed by the recent high of $90 billion in 1986. Due to yen appreciation, it fell back to $60 billion in 1989. But most forecasts, both

Japanese and foreign, predict that trade surpluses will continue swelling in coming years and perhaps indefinitely.

Large and expanding Japanese surpluses naturally reflect large and expanding deficits of other countries. The United States suffered a record deficit of $21 billion in fiscal 1983, followed by even larger ones in later years. In 1989, it was a depressing $43 billion. But it was not alone. The European Community ran a deficit of $19 billion in 1989, and Southeast Asia was $21 billion in the red in the same year. Deficits occurred in other places, including Africa and Latin America. For them as well, forecasts indicate more deficits to come unless something can arrest the trend.

The deficits inevitably focused attention on both sides of the trade equation. The situation for Japan's exports was quite clear. Its manufacturers produced goods of excellent quality at reasonable prices that were welcomed by consumers the world over. It was easy for Japanese companies to get into most markets and sell directly or through the existing channels. Their success was shown by booming sales and rising market shares—and often by trade friction and surpluses.[2]

This provoked a negative reaction abroad, but one that was partly understandable and bound to intensify if nothing corrected the imbalances. It took the form of an increasing number of trade barriers to protect endangered domestic industries such as textiles, steel, shipbuilding, automobiles, and electronics. Soon there were broader demands for protectionism in many circles. While the principle of free trade was not renounced, it was certainly infringed more and more.[3] And there were repeated calls for something that was significantly different, namely "fair trade."

The other side of the equation was not as readily perceptible. It was maintained by foreign companies that they also offered good products at reasonable prices and that more of them should be sold in Japan. Such claims were made at both ends of the spectrum, among high-tech firms in advanced countries and simpler ones in developing nations whose labor costs were very low. These companies had been able to sell their goods in international markets and often competed successfully against Japanese goods in third countries. Yet, whenever they tried to enter the Japanese market, they encountered exceptional difficulties and made little headway.[4]

This failure was revealed by the trade statistics. Japan not only imported less than it exported, it imported proportionately less manufactures than other countries at the same economic level. The share of manufactured goods in total imports was only 49 percent in 1988, compared to 75 percent for Germany, 80 percent for Great Britain and 82 percent for the United States.[5] The situation was even more striking with regard to manufactured imports as a percent of gross domestic product. It was under three percent for Japan at the same time that it exceeded seven percent for the United States, 14 percent for Germany, and 17 percent for Great Britain.[6] Admittedly, there had been some increase in the share of manufactured imports over the years, but it was much smaller than elsewhere, and sizable gaps remained.

Within these imports, which were less than exports, and within the manufactured goods, which were at lower levels than other advanced countries, there was a third anomaly. The share of consumer goods was a mere 20 percent and sometimes less. Most other manufactures were either capital goods or intermediate goods, namely products that helped Japan generate its own finished products and machinery. This meant that the outlook for future progress was bleak since Japanese companies were still gearing up to replace imported articles.

It therefore became urgent to seek the cause of this inability to sell more goods in general, and more manufactured (and especially consumer) goods in particular. In so doing, its partners gradually realized that Japan had also been protecting its market, not always in the same ways as others but certainly using methods that were equally effective. Indeed, on closer inspection it appeared to many that Japan had the most closed and impenetrable market of the liberal economies. This was steadfastly denied by the government and business leaders, but it was evident that barriers were present and had to be eliminated to facilitate access.

Notes

1. Ministry of Finance. Japanese trade statistics are on a customs-clearance basis and do not always coincide with comparable figures collected by its various trading partners.

2. See I.M. Destler and Hideo Sato, eds., *Coping with U.S.- Japanese Economic Conflicts*, (Lexington: D.C. Heath, 1982), Edward J. Lincoln, *Japan's Unequal Trade*, (Washington, D.C., Brookings Institution, 1990), Clyde V. Prestowitz, Jr., *Trading Places*, (New York: Basic Books, 1988), and Jon Woronoff, *World Trade War*, (New York: Praeger, 1984), pp. 108-84.

3. See Woronoff, op. cit., pp. 218-55.

4. Ibid., pp. 55-107.

5. OECD, *Statistics of Foreign Trade*.

6. See Lincoln, op. cit., pp. 18-25.

③

Impediments, Ordinary

When foreign business executives and governments began seeking the causes of their difficulties in penetrating the Japanese market, there was no shortage of impediments to be found.[1] In fact, it soon turned out that there were several different levels of difficulties. It was rare that just one obstacle had to be overcome. Behind it was another, and often yet another. The comparisons most often made were to speak of the layers of an onion or a castle with its surrounding fortifications.

The outside layer or external fortification was the rather common and conventional one of tariffs and quotas. After the war, Japanese industry had grown up behind a whole battery of such mechanisms. Even in the mid-1960s, the effective customs tariff rate was as much as 21 percent. This was considerably higher than in other advanced countries at the time. The number of import restrictions was also substantial, 50 for manufactured goods and 60 for agricultural goods.

Gradually, these conventional barriers were brought down. But, like its counterparts, the Japanese government was selective, so that those that had little practical purpose were reduced first while others were preserved until the bitter end. This left towering peaks even when the general level was much lower.[2]

Examples of selective protection included the automotive industry, where the abolition of quotas on passenger cars came only in 1966, at which time tariffs remained as high as 35 to 40 percent. Long after tariffs on computers were reduced, those for peripherals stayed high. This effort to protect such major industries was more understandable than some others. The tariffs on confectionaries, alcoholic beverages, and processed foods were also inexplicably high. And there were strict quotas on leather and leather footwear.

Behind the tariffs and quotas—sometimes already in place, sometimes raised as the former came down—were the nontariff barriers (NTBs). This sort of impediment is in place in just about every trading nation. But NTBs have never taken on such a varied and ingenious nature, applying to just about any product under the sun, nor were they ever more prolific than they are in Japan.[3]

Those NTBs that had the most defensible basis were related to product and health safety. They were particularly dense in the sectors of foodstuffs and pharmaceuticals.[4] But NTBs often seemed to exceed any reasonable bounds. For example, in addition to clinical retesting of new drugs, it was necessary to repeat the preclinical testing in Japan. This meant tests that are normally run on white mice in laboratories had to be redone at great cost in time and money. Even more frivolous was the requirement that mineral water be pasteurized by heating.[5]

While the safety requirements often made sense, the procedures were unnecessarily complicated. It was obligatory to test exceptionally large numbers, for exceptionally long times, under exceptionally arduous conditions. Test certificates already obtained from national authorities were not accepted, and thus the whole process had to be repeated. It was not possible to have the testing done locally; it had to be done after the goods arrived in Japan. In some cases, every single article (for example, each individual car) had to be tested. Things dragged on further because inspectors were too few or too slow.

For goods where standards were applicable, often the Japanese standards favored domestic manufactures. It was necessary to use the same techniques and design when others were equally effective. Some of the requirements were petty and obviously biased against competing foreign products, especially those concerning size, weight, or material. This included regulations that made it hard to sell foreign lumber or plywood.

What was worse, the standards were sometimes modified at very short notice . . . for foreigners at least. It therefore turned out that a product that had been sold on the Japanese market was no longer acceptable.[6] Even more absurd, when a product was improved it had to undergo all the formalities and testing another time and could not be sold until they were completed. Finally, the certificates of approval were usually given to the local agent and not the foreign manufacturer—and if the agent changed, the manufacturer had to go through the whole process all over again.

In addition to bone fide standards—which at least were on paper—there were many others that were imparted by verbal suggestions of the local officials in the form of "administrative guidance." These were usually unclear and at times were disclosed only to domestic manufacturers. Foreigners were then excepted to meet conditions that had never been explained to them and could be found in no book. The most striking case of this was a limitation on the ingredients that could be used for cosmetics, only some of which were indicated to foreigners while many more were known and used by Japanese. Also, while not compulsory, it was helpful for goods to bear supposed quality marks like JAS and SG, which few foreign products could obtain.

Government officials and bureaucrats imposed many other handicaps.[7] Customs inspectors tended to be overly meticulous in checking whether imported goods met all the conditions. This could take the form of time-consuming checks in which the slightest, inconsequential failing could result in rejection. What was particularly unpleasant was that it was impossible to get a ruling as to why a rejection occurred; often goods rejected at one point might be cleared at another point.

Other forms of bureaucratic intervention were unique to and exceedingly important in the Japanese context. Some arose from the practice of industrial policy and targeting by certain ministries. In this, the ministry would provide specific incentives and broad support to local companies, which put them at an advantage over foreign competitors. This included all sorts of tax rebates, accelerated depreciation of equipment, aid in acquiring technologies and raw materials, and so on. Another aspect was research and development carried out by public bodies and then put at the disposal of selected manufacturers. The best known examples were to upgrade the quality of Japanese computers.

In addition to support, however, there was also protection. As soon as it was determined to promote an "infant industry," barriers went up to preserve the market until demand could be met by local companies. This protection included tariffs, quotas, and NTBs and was supplemented by government or other purchases. Only after the industry could fend for itself was most of the protection removed—but it could be restored if the sector encountered difficulties or went into a decline. Measures for ailing industries involved cartels and other means for restricting competing imports.

Industrial policy has been practiced most systematically by the Ministry of International Trade and Industry (MITI) for a broad range of sectors. Its role was substantial earlier on for coal, iron and steel, light metals, chemicals and petrochemicals, automobiles, electronics, and computers. Nowadays it backs biotechnology, new materials, atomic energy, and aerospace. But MITI is not the only example. Similar activities are undertaken by the Ministry of Health to promote the pharmaceutical and medical equipment industries; the Ministry of Agriculture cultivates the farm machinery sector even more strongly; the Science and Technology Agency helps some high-tech areas; and so on.

From the outset, the government engaged in a "buy Japan" policy that was not so different from the analogous policies abroad. Yet, even after rules on opening procurement were adopted, the government was slow to enforce them. Local governments tended to overlook these agreements, and semigovernmental agencies regularly ignored them. This included the Japanese National Railways (JNR), the Tobacco Monopoly, and especially Nippon Telegraph and Telephone (NTT).

The amounts of money involved here were tremendous. Even more significant was the way contracting occurred on the basis of negotiated prices rather than open bidding. This made it possible to help a company launch a product by guaranteeing a market. This was done most extensively for telecommunications equipment and computers by NTT. JNR obtained its rolling stock locally even when competitive goods existed abroad. The most extreme case was, of course, to create a domestic cigarette industry that could flourish only in the absence of imports.

Foreign direct investment was restricted even more thoroughly than imports. For two decades after the war, foreigners were prevented from investing in numerous sectors that were regarded either as unessential (most consumer goods) or strategic and reserved for Japanese (agriculture, real estate, computers, petrochemicals, nuclear energy, aircraft and space, etc.). Even in permitted sectors, they were only allowed to own less than 50 percent of a joint venture they established and 25 percent of an existing Japanese company. Only in those areas where the Japanese sought products or technology was it somewhat easier to invest. Moreover, even when the law provided that investment was permitted, foreign businessmen faced considerable bureaucratic red tape and occasional pressure.[8]

Admittedly, none of the barriers or measures were unknown abroad. But they were never as extensively used or as deeply embedded, nor as effective in blocking imports and investment. They also remained in place long after most other advanced countries had liberalized.

Notes

1. American Chamber of Commerce in Japan, *Report on Trade Barriers, Membership Survey*, Tokyo, 1982.

2. See Michael Blaker, ed., The Politics of Trade: US and *Japanese Policy Making for the GATT Negotiations* (New York: Columbia University Press, 1978).

3. Arthur D. Little, *The Japanese Non-Tariff Barrier Issue*, Tokyo, 1979.

4. Kearney International, *Non-Tariff Barriers Affecting the Health Care Industry in Japan*, Tokyo, 1980.

5. For an analysis of nontariff barriers in the pharmaceutical, cosmetics, food-stuffs, and automotive industries, see Jon Woronoff, *Inside Japan, Inc.*, (Tokyo: Lotus Press, 1982), pp. 131-65.

6. Frank A. Weil and Norman D. Glick, "Japan—Is the Market Open?" *Law and Policy in International Business*, Vol. 11, No. 3, 1979.

7. American Chamber of Commerce in Japan, op. cit.

8. On this period, see Dan Fenno Henderson, *Foreign Enterprises in Japan*, (Tokyo: Tuttle, 1975).

CHAPTER

4

Getting in Step

Slowly but surely, each of the layers was peeled from the onion or the fortifications battered down, depending on the preferred metaphor. But it was a long, drawn-out process that has now been going on for over three decades, although that is frequently forgotten. It has passed through several spurts of activity, with the first big push coming in the mid-1960s, a second in the late 1970s, a third in the mid-1980s, and a forth at present.

Shortly after World War II, it was felt that Japan might not be able to rebuild and become a modern industrial economy again. Japan was therefore allowed to adopt rather strict measures to that end, and its use of "infant industry" protection was initially accepted. It was even tolerated much later as the country began to expand and export. Only when its exports became irksome was it realized that Japan had outgrown the old methods and should be held to the same conduct as other advanced countries. This decision was consecrated by Japan's acceptance of Article VIII of the International Monetary Fund and entry into the Organization for Economic Cooperation and Development (OECD) and the General Agreement on Tariffs and Trade (GATT) as of 1963.

This initiated a series of moves that was reinforced by the Kennedy Round of multilateral trade negotiations of 1964-67. Customs tariffs fell sharply from 21 percent in 1966 to 10 percent in 1973 and to 5 percent in 1974, which was comparable to other advanced nations.[1] The average dropped further in the early 1980s, thanks to the Tokyo Round and special efforts to accelerate its implementation. By now, Japan's level is much lower than that of the United States or of the European Community.

The same process occurred for quotas. There were as many as 460 import restrictions in 1962. By the end of the decade, this had decreased to 110. In 1975, most were discarded, and only 27 residual items remain, of which just five were for manufactured goods. But it has been hard to remove the last few despite strong urging from abroad, and they are disappearing only slowly. Still, in its defense, Japan can point out that most European countries are far worse.

The scenario was similar for investment. Restrictions were removed only slowly, in stages, and under pressure from the OECD. First, foreign companies were allowed to convert yen earnings into foreign exchange. Then, as of 1967, more and more sectors were taken off the restricted list. By the early 1970s, foreigners were permitted to hold a larger share of the ownership in joint ventures, staring with 50 percent in 1971 and 100 percent (for all but crucial sectors) in 1973. Finally, under the Foreign Exchange Control Law of 1980, nearly all sectors were opened entirely, although acquisitions in strategic companies had to be approved. Again, although much later than the rest, Japan has gotten in step.

The struggle to eliminate nontariff barriers made little progress until the early 1980s, although individual business executives or working parties like the U.S.-Japan Trade Study Group revealed their presence and unfairness. It was only the growing trade imbalances and ensuing friction that led the governments to tackle these more intricate and delicate items—which were more visible than ever now that many tariffs had come down. Unlike the situation with GATT for tariffs and quotas, there was no suitable machinery to deal with NTBs. This meant that Japan's trading partners could do little more than complain and threaten. This ultimately proved effective, as Japan was dependent on trade and eager to demonstrate its cooperativeness.

For a long time, the very existence of NTBs was strenuously denied by the Japanese government. Then, in 1982, there was a breakthrough. The Esaki Committee, appointed by the Liberal Democratic Party, examined 99 alleged NTBs and conceded that 67 of them did exist. Gradually, the government was forced to admit that there were considerably more. It was aided in this task of uncovering NTBs by foreign businesses, which now felt freer to express their grievances.

Thus, during the 1980s, NTBs were painstakingly removed, one after the other, although some new ones cropped up. Even more important, it was recognized that broader measures had to be taken as well. It was necessary to increase the transparency of the standard-setting exercise so that outsiders would know exactly what the standards were in good time. Indeed, on occasion they might participate in bodies that set these standards. Foreigners could also receive certain quality marks, and more foreign data and tests could be accepted while additional inspectors were posted abroad.

Government ministries and agencies were also called on to make things clearer and simpler for foreign businesses. To solve any possible problems, a special Office of the Trade Ombudsman was set up to receive complaints and look into their justification. It could coordinate the efforts of all bodies so that any difficulties might be quickly overcome. The individual administrations also provided more help and advice than before. While much remained to be done, the bureaucracy did become somewhat more responsive.

Government procurement was progressively opened at both the central and local levels, although not as much or as rapidly as had been hoped.[2] Much more promising, the semigovernmental agencies that had the biggest budgets and had been most difficult in the past were undergoing privatization. It was assumed that, once subject to market forces, they would have to buy the best and cheapest goods available. This occurred first with the Tobacco Monopoly and Nippon Telegraph and Telephone and then the Japanese National Railways.

Meanwhile, industrial policy had become almost an embarrassment to the Japanese government, which tried not to engage in spectacular R & D projects or, if so, to see that some foreign companies participated.[3] More generally, there were relatively fewer new industries to be promoted by MITI or other bodies, although there is no doubt that aerospace enjoys some protection and sales of foreign satellites and rockets are hurt. Where the most serious problems remain are with regard to the ailing industries that are still supported by MITI, including aluminum, pulp and paper, and petrochemicals.

While most of these advances were piecemeal, they were presented within the framework of a series of "market-opening" packages, which were adopted by the government with much fanfare. They included further reductions in tariffs, elimination of quotas, fairer standards and inspection, greater procurement of foreign goods, more transparency in administrative action, and so on. There were literally dozens of these packages and assorted individual measures, the most impressive being a broad-based "action program" launched by Prime Minister Nakasone in 1985. Each one was presented as the "last," in the sense that henceforth the market or specific sector was fully open and nothing more remained to be done. But they were all followed by further foreign complaints and pressure and, in due course, further efforts to open the market.

Since general measures did not seem to be achieving the desired results, the United States government shifted to a product-by-product approach. This was called MOSS (market-oriented sector specific) and talks were held at the highest level from 1984 to 1986.[4] The sectors concerned were telecommunications, medical equipment and pharmaceuticals, electronics, and forest products, all areas in which American companies were strongly competitive but had had little success in penetrating the market. There were also specific negotiations on sales of American semiconductors and participation of American contractors in public works projects and later on, under the "Super 301," on satellites, forest products, and supercomputers.[5]

Despite official agreements, progress was often painfully slow and frustration grew. Observers complained that many measures were too selective, liberalizing products of lesser importance while still protecting more essential ones. The implementation was called into question. Some promises remained purely verbal because no machinery was created to put them into practice. In other cases, it was clear that even if there were a formal commitment at higher levels, there was a lack of goodwill further down among the ordinary bureaucrats who had to apply the measures. And, of course, it was repeatedly lamented that old barriers were simply replaced by new ones.

Increasingly, critics insisted that the "proof of the pudding is in the eating." This signified that the only way of showing that the liberalization was meaningful was for the trade situation to change dramatically, namely, for many more foreign products to be sold in Japan. Alas, there was little evidence that things were improving in this sense. The share of manufactures imports remained well below the levels elsewhere and, while imports expanded, exports were growing more rapidly. Trade imbalances not only remained large, they grew implacably. And most forecasts indicated even more bloated imbalances to come.[6]

That is why American Congressmen, led by Senator John Danforth, began working on another, more radical approach known as "reciprocity." Partly, it involved turning free trade into "fair" trade, whereby Japan should make its market as open as that of the United States. It was urged to promptly remove all barriers and create a "level playing field." If that did not materialize, then Japan should be prevented from exporting more to the United States, thereby balancing trade artificially. While reciprocity was discussed at length, specific legislation was never adopted. But individual acts were taken to limit Japanese exports of various products, including steel and automobiles, through voluntary restraint. This was a distinct move toward "managed" trade, one that was criticized by Western free traders and Japanese businessmen, but tacitly approved by MITI officials.

Obviously, reciprocity and managed trade were not as beneficial as expanded two-way trade and, in addition, not in keeping with GATT and other rules. So, to better balance trade, American Congressmen pushed for sales quotas of American goods, an idea that never became official policy but was vaguely incorporated in the semiconductor agreement. Again, both free traders and the Japanese objected. While it was reasonable to ask that the market be opened, it was improper to insist that foreigners get a specific share of that market. After all, foreign companies might not be supplying products that were good or cheap enough to be bought widely, or they might not be making sufficient efforts to sell them.

Fair or not, it was clear that the conflicts would not be resolved until more foreign companies were successful and the Japanese market actually absorbed enough foreign goods to improve both the trade balance and political relations.

Notes

1. *KKC Brief No. 29* (Tokyo: Keizai Koho Center, July 1985).
2. Chikara Higashi, *Japanese Trade Policy Formulation* (New York: Praeger, 1983), pp. 106-14.
3. Ministry of International Trade and Industry, *Background Information on Japan's Industrial Policy*, May 1983.
4. Lincoln, op. cit., pp. 148-53 and Prestowitz, op. cit., pp. 296-99.
5. Prestowitz, op. cit., pp. 26-70.
6. *Far Eastern Economic Review*, June 21, 1990, pp. 92-93.

CHAPTER

5

Impediments, Extraordinary

It slowly dawned on most observers that the reasons things were not improving was not so much that goods were blocked by a series of impediments: tariffs and quotas, nontariff barriers and bureaucratic hassles, government procurement, and industrial policy. It was not that the market-opening measures were poorly implemented or partially counteracted. It was not even that Japanese goods were so superior that foreign ones could not compete. It was that further, uncharted barriers remained.

After peeling away all the layers, after taking all the outlying fortifications, there was still something more. This something was never clearly articulated or accurately grasped, but it was becoming increasingly evident that the place to look was in the distribution system. Here, there were two primary elements that had to be taken into account: the complex and unwieldy nature of the system itself and the special relationships that arose between various agents in the distribution process.

Foreign businesses in Japan had long been aware of these problems and occasionally complained to their governments. But it took some time for the politicians and bureaucrats to realize just how important such barriers could be. Eventually, they grasped that it was impossible to sell even the finest goods if they could not get onto the store shelves or into the display rooms. And it served little purpose to dismantle tariffs and quotas, NTBs and red tape, government procurement, and the rest if special relationships between local businesses discouraged imports.

Still, in 1982 the U.S. Department of Commerce did list the distribution system among the obstacles to trade. In particular, it pointed out that it could be considered a "non-tariff barrier to imports." The difficulties derived "from a complex, somewhat archaic system that, particularly with regard to consumer goods, evolved over time to meet the particular needs of the domestic market. Criticism of the Japanese distribution system often focuses on the very high retail prices of imported goods." Awareness of the role of intercompany relations was more nebulous. It was merely noted that "cartel-like activity among Japanese firms can limit access to distribution channels."[1]

Once again, the Japanese authorities—governmental and especially business—denied any such barriers or disadvantages for foreign traders. They were pointedly dismissed in a statement of the Japan Federation of Economic Organizations (Keidanren), the principal voice of the business community:

> The myth persists that business relations in Japan are fixed and unchanging, that transactions among members of a group predominate, and that the market is difficult to penetrate, even with superior products to offer. In fact, however, intragroup business deals are not common. The Japanese market is simply too competitive to allow success based on dependence on special trading relationships. There is also loud criticism of the Japanese distribution system, but studies have made it clear that, while much room remains for improvement, the system itself does not discriminate against foreign goods.[2]

Yet, some of the complaints were hard to refute. Even the Economic Planning Agency had to admit the complications of the distribution system. A 1984 report indicated that the distribution routes were more than three times longer than in the United States and Europe, and the productivity per employee in the wholesale and retail sectors was only two-thirds that of the United States.[3] Numerous polls showed that consumers regarded the prices of imported goods as excessively high, and there was no doubt that multilayered channels and large margins accounted for some of that.[4] And a joint study by the U.S. and Japanese governments showed that two out of three products were more expensive in Japan.[5] Also, the activities of the major industrial groups and keiretsu were a basic fact of business life.

Thus, it was obvious that something had to be done. But what? Most of the distribution and other commercial arrangements were traditional and had become an integral part of the economic scene. It would be most difficult to change them effectively and, with some justice, the Japanese insisted that they had a right to their own business culture. The financial connections, on the other hand, were frequently more important than any customs and practices and were occasionally of a dubious nature. To the extent that this did discriminate against their nationals, foreign governments might feel compelled to complain or exert political pressure. But there was little more they could do since none of this came under GATT or other international agreements.

Perhaps conceding the difficulty of entering the market, the Japanese government did attempt to ease the process in certain ways. As of the early 1980s, it launched "buy foreign" campaigns. Special "import fairs" were held in which foreign products would be displayed in various parts of Japan. "Import-buying missions" were sent abroad to purchase foreign goods. The most spectacular gesture by Prime Minister Nakasone when presenting his "action program" was to make a special appeal to the Japanese public to buy more foreign articles. MITI subsequently asked major companies to set ambitious targets for imports. The Japan External Trade Organization (JETRO) opened special import desks in its overseas offices and held import shows in Japan. And, to cap it all, the special trade committee including top politicians, bureaucrats, and businessmen set up an "import board" in 1990.

But this could be of only subsidiary use. The import missions purchased only limited quantities of goods, often those which would have been bought anyway. The fairs and shows introduced products to the market but did nothing to facilitate their passage through the existing channels. The Japanese became more benevolent importers rather than giving foreign companies what they really wanted, a chance to sell more of their goods normally. And consumers, who did like foreign products, still found it cheaper to buy them abroad.

All else having failed, the United States introduced a Structural Impediments Initiative (SII) that looked into more informal or cultural barriers that made the Japanese market so hard to crack. These included an inefficient distribution system, rigidities in the pricing mechanism, exclusionary business practices, problems of *keiretsu* groupings, high land prices, and inadequate social investment. To back it up, Japan was warned that it could be named a "structurally unfair" trading nation under the provisions of the 1988 Trade Act and subjected to the penalties of the Super 301 clause. Alas, after a year of desultory negotiations, little was accomplished other than to revise the law limiting large retail stores, modify the land tax system, increase somewhat the monitoring of *keiretsu* ties and boost the public works budget.[6]

Thus, the distribution system contains the ultimate and most decisive barriers, and within that system, the links between groupings further restrict the influx of foreign products. Although there have been some changes, and more are periodically promised, it is still very difficult for foreigners to operate in the Japanese structure. It is, therefore, essential to know just what the difficulties are and how they can be coped with.

Notes

1. United States Congress, *Hearings before the Committee on Foreign Affairs, House of Representatives*, Washington D.C.: Government Printing Office, March-August 1982.

2. *KCC Brief No. 26* (Tokyo: Keizai Koho Center, February 1985), p. 1.

3. *Japan Economic Journal*, June 26, 1984.

4. "Imported Goods Still Dear; Consumers Balk," *Daily Yomiuri*, April 15, 1985, p. 2.

5. *Daily Yomiuri*, November 9, 1889.

6. *Far Eastern Economic Review*, July 12, 1990, pp. 63-65.

Corporate Connections

C H A P T E R

6

The Inescapable Groupings

It can hardly be stressed enough that every business community has its own characteristic features. Some commercial practices and legal institutions encountered in one place may not be found, or may appear only in a somewhat different form, elsewhere. Others that are generally lacking abroad may be of particular significance in a specific country. Given its lengthy autonomous growth remote from Western culture and its periodic phases of isolation and nationalism, it is hardly surprising that the differences in Japan should be notable despite any real or apparent resemblance to the West.

One of the most striking differences, when properly understood, is the extent to which markets are organized and structured in certain ways by units that are sometimes called *keiretsu*, if more formal, and merely groups or groupings if less so. These are "alignments" or combinations of companies, more or less closely related and coordinated, that do business with one another on a regular—and often quite intimate—basis.

Three basic categories of groupings should be carefully considered. One is the most traditional type, which is most frequently called *keiretsu*, and consists of a number of companies in diverse sectors that revolve around one of the leading banks. This is often referred to as a horizontal grouping or capital *keiretsu* because of the close financial ties. Another derives from the supplier networks created by dynamic manufacturers, commonly known as a vertical grouping or enterprise *keiretsu* because it is dominated by a strong company. The third is referred to as a distribution *keiretsu* since it brings together a manufacturer and its sales outlets. These various groupings play an extremely important role in the Japanese economy. It is hardly possible to do business in Japan, as a local or foreign entity, without running into them as buyers or sellers, clients or suppliers, allies or rivals. Yet their formation, organization, and activities have been inadequately explored in the literature and, what is worse, poorly grasped by those unaccustomed to doing business the Japanese way.

This is an attempt to describe the various categories of groupings, see who belongs to some of the most important ones, and examine how they operate. It is impossible to tell everything in this or perhaps any book, for these groupings engage in exceptionally varied and extensive activities. Moreover, these units are sufficiently flexible and adaptable for their action to vary from case to case and over time. Finally, much of what they do is not generally disclosed to the public. Still, even a brief introduction can be of help.

In studying the groupings, especially if labeled with the increasingly unflattering name of *keiretsu*, it is essential to keep some balance. It would be unwise to ignore their activities or write them off as mere remnants of the past. It would be no less foolish to exaggerate the closeness of their links or their ability to throw up barriers to outsiders. This being said, a good look at these groupings is vital for any proper comprehension of Japanese business.

Just which combinations can be classified as *keiretsu* or groupings is sometimes difficult to determine since there are varying degrees of cooperation and considerable nuances in how they operate. It is generally agreed that there are eight major capital *keiretsu* and many other smaller ones, Toyo Keizai listing as as many as 40.[1] While there are large numbers of vertical groupings, since subcontracting is so widespread, there are only several dozen of particular note. As for the distribution *keiretsu*, they are even more limited because it has proven harder to structure (or restructure) marketing channels in the face of resistance from existing distributors.

While the number of groupings is modest, several things must be remembered. First of all, each group can have many members. Some major *keiretsu* have accumulated a hundred or more. Just the eight top horizontal groupings are estimated by a leading authority to have over a thousand members, and this only for those that are closely involved. The largest vertical grouping, that of Nippon Steel, numbers about 200. And, of course, each one of these members has its own subsidiaries, suppliers, and other dependents. This creates very extensive "families" of companies that can be related to one another.

However, they are not just any companies. Those participating in the groups are often the largest and most prestigious. In fact, the ones that will be mentioned further on form almost a "who's who" of Japanese business. Among the horizontal groupings are names like Mitsubishi, Mitsui, Sumitomo, Dai-Ichi Kangyo Bank (DKB), Industrial Bank of Japan (IBJ), and so on. Vertical groupings have been created by Hitachi, Matsushita and Sony, Toyota, Nissan and Honda, Nippon Steel, and more. Some of these also possess distribution *keiretsu*.

Beyond the name and prestige, it is essential to remember that these organizations also have tremendous economic power. The eight largest horizontal groupings account for 21 percent of the total paid up capital, 17 percent of total annual sales, and six percent of the total labor force—despite the fact that they represent only 0.04 percent of all companies in Japan. [2] A typology of the major groupings and the relations between them is provided in Figure 6.1.

Moreover, as groups, they are among the largest business entities in the world. The banks that form the core of the leading capital *keiretsu* are all among the top 20 internationally, and Dai-Ichi Kangyo is number one worldwide. Toyota and Nissan are the third and sixth ranking automobile companies, Hitachi and Matsushita are the third and fourth biggest electronics makers, Nippon Steel is first in its sector. While other producers are somewhat less prominent, they are all rapidly catching up.

Finally, while such groupings do not prevail in all sectors, they are encountered in a fair number, including some of the most attractive. The horizontal *keiretsu* are deeply involved in services like banking, insurance, transport, and trading. They also engage in manufacturing. Vertical groupings are most noticeable in the automotive, electronics, steel, and shipbuilding industries. Distribution *keiretsu* exist for sales of automobiles, electronics, cosmetics, and pharmaceuticals. Even if less significant in other branches, the groupings do play some part in textiles and garments, household appliances, and even foodstuffs.

Considering the tremendous impact close relations can have on the way companies operate, it is essential to determine even roughly their effect on the Japanese economy. This has become a controversial question in recent years. It was once admitted quite freely by Japanese officials and academics that the various *keiretsu* and groupings were not only numerous and influential but also a basic foundation of the economic structure. Since they have come under fire by Japan's trading partners as a possible barrier, their existence has been played down and occasionally almost denied by the authorities.[3]

But there can be little doubt as to their existence. What is more questionable is just how meaningful and effective the links are and, more pertinent, to what extent they influence behavior so as to restrict access to the market and distort economic forces. The reasons for uncertainty are many. After all, while such relations will move companies to do business together, even then they will work with outside firms if products are not available within the group or if outside suppliers offer better prices, quality, or service. The links thus encourage commercial transactions but do not guarantee them, and insiders benefit from certain advantages but not complete acceptance.

Figure 6.1
Relations between Industrial Groups

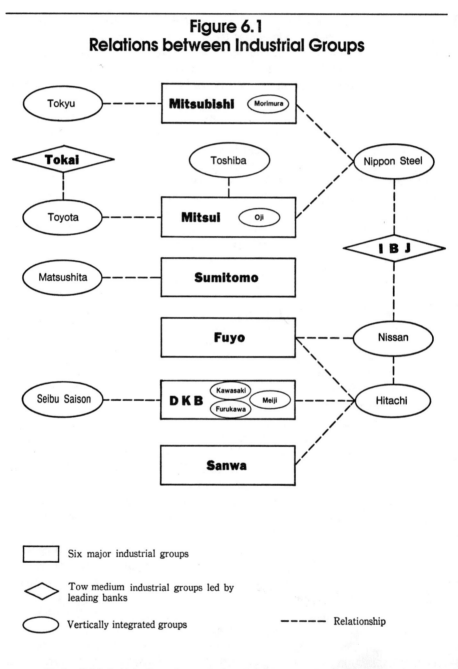

CREDIT: Dodwell Marketing Consultants, *Industrial Groupings In Japan*, 1988, p. 5.

Moreover, while some companies are part of one grouping or another, many more are completely or largely independent. The *keiretsu* and groupings englobe only about one percent of all companies, leaving 99 percent to work by different rules. On the other hand, that one percent includes the largest and most dynamic companies, and they have a disproportionately large share of the nation's capital, sales, work force, and so on. Other firms tend to copy the groupings in at least some aspects since their influence on the business culture is so pervasive.

Thus, one can speak of the *keiretsu* as being typical and distinctive. But it is crucial that this be understood correctly and not be exaggerated. While there are certainly more such units in Japan, they are only one form of organization. Similar units and practices exist in other countries. The conglomerates are a case in point. Groups of this sort are more prevalent in some developing countries and parts of Western Europe than in the United States (though it was noticeable even in the United States in earlier years). The reasons why such groupings are less active abroad derive from differing historical, cultural, and social conditions, especially a more individualistic people and a more entrepreneurial business culture. But it can be traced as clearly to more effective antitrust legislation.

Bonds That Hold

As indicated, these groupings assume quite different functions and can be subdivided into three categories: horizontal, vertical, and distribution *keiretsu*. Such a distinction is made for reasons of readier comprehension, since the activities vary considerably. But it should not be forgotten that all companies possess several functions, and thus one company may well fit into more than one category. It may, for example, be part of a banking alignment and also have its own integrated supplier network, or it may subcontract work and also control part of the distribution network.

Thus, the distinctions are described here largely to clarify their modus operandi. They should not cloud the fact that there are also many similarities between the groupings. In certain ways, they are just differing aspects or manifestations of the same underlying phenomenon. After all, some of the motives for such organization are rooted in ancient Japanese traditions, social customs, and mind-sets that affect many other features of the economy as well, most notably wholesale and retail distribution. Indeed, as soon as they are mentioned, it will be apparent that their impact is even broader and shapes, among other things, management techniques, social institutions, and even politics.

An overriding concern for many Japanese businesses is loyalty and related thereto, stability. It is therefore regarded as advantageous to create a more structured framework for business activities—for example, closer and steadier relations between manufacturers and suppliers or between manufacturers and distributors. This spawns the long-standing and time-honored relationships many

Japanese take pride in. However, while less readily admitted, it also creates certain inefficiencies and restrictions that will be referred to later.

Of course, even in Japan it takes more than mere sentiment to forge solid and lasting ties. This has been noticed more by the locals than by most outside observers. The companies involved have created all sorts of links that bind them to one another in an equal-to-equal or superior-inferior relationship. It is impossible to comprehend the effectiveness (or at least solidity) and the workings of the companies concerned, without noting this aspect.

One link, the most visible, is through shareholding. In the horizontal groupings that bring together companies that are largely autonomous and roughly on an equal footing, this can take the form of cross-shareholding. Even then, there is a predominance of ownership emanating from certain core units such as banks, insurance firms, or trading companies. In the vertical groupings and distribution *keiretsu*, ownership is usually held by the parent company. The degree of ownership can range from majority to 100 percent, making the lesser body a mere affiliate or subsidiary; to less than 50 percent, giving the company reasonable leeway; to a few percent, which is little more than a token of interest.

Other connections are created by an exchange of personnel. Once again, this can be between loosely related companies on an equal footing, but it is far more prevalent in the case of vertical groupings and distribution *keiretsu*. Those transferred, seconded, or retired out to other firms, especially subsidiaries, can be at the top. This is done through the appointment of directors to related companies and, no less crucial, appointments of managers, auditors, or sales executives. At a lower level, this can consist of "lending" ordinary sales help to retail outlets. Given the importance of human relations in Japanese society, this subtler form of interpenetration can be extremely effective.

Some of the groupings are sufficiently structured and coordinated to have common bodies, such as the presidents' clubs of horizontal groupings. Others limit their contacts to periodic and sometimes quite informal meetings. But the vertical groupings and distribution *keiretsu*, given their ownership and direction, bring the subsidiaries (and also independent suppliers and outlets) into particularly tight units or exercise control in other ways. Another form of cooperation is for several bodies to launch joint ventures in which closer coordination than usual occurs, albeit for specific projects.

Financial connections are obviously important as well. Bank loans to group members and purchases of stocks by banks and insurance companies are just the most visible forms. This is done to encourage group members to deal not only with the lenders but also to deal with one another, since all are probably borrowers. Large companies also help smaller ones financially. Trading companies lend to their suppliers and offer credit to their customers. Manufacturers guarantee loans for lesser suppliers and subcontractors who cannot provide adequate collateral.

The mere fact of doing business together for years has its influence. It is not only a question of knowing one another personally; suppliers have come to know the exact needs of their clients and cater to them most devotedly. They get considerable feedback without which no competitor would know what is desired. If the relationship is such that a large portion (perhaps all) of their sales is directed to one or several group members, they would think twice before leaving it. They would also think twice before dealing with a rival, even if for one article it offered better terms.

Finally, although it is hard to put one's finger on, there is a common ethos among the companies and their personnel. After all, they frequently sport the same badge and trademark and inspire a common image. Members keenly feel that they are part of a distinct group of companies, something that is essential in a society where employees relate so closely to their workplace and regard themselves more as company people than free agents who can sell their skills anywhere. This encourages them to help one another and cooperate in various ways, many of which are hard to define but can have significant impact.

This social and psychological element must always be borne in mind when one is tempted to write off the *keiretsu* due to a lack of mechanical ties. Some have claimed that *keiretsu* cannot be effective because, often enough, there is no centralized organization, or the crossholding is minor, or the companies have other sources of finance and clients. Wiser counsel comes from an expert on the subject, Dan Fenno Henderson: "The *keiretsu*, which is in organizational principle little more than a confederation, is uniquely effective in Japan because of the familial insider-outsider psychology and the efficacy of conciliar decision-making techniques. In Japan, these can mold an operable unit from such an unlikely organizational pattern."[4]

Similar causes naturally have similar effects. Companies that are members of groupings will work more closely together. Part of this is almost spontaneous since firms are closely related and their employees have a greater chance of knowing each other. Another part, probably the larger, results from design. The *keiretsu* and groupings were not created merely for social intercourse but for business purposes. They were carefully put together so that firms that complement one another's activities can cooperate to their mutual benefit.

The outcome has been a good deal of business flowing from one group member to another. In some cases, it is a relatively minor share of total sales that comes from other group members; in others, the level is significant. This is particularly true of the enterprise groupings, which generate much of the necessary supplies internally. It also applies to a lesser extent to the distribution *keiretsu*, which sell a large share of the products. It is least significant among the horizontal *keiretsu*, which include members in a wide variety of fields, some of which have little to do with one another.

Statistics are hard to come by since many figures are not disclosed, especially as relates to transactions between subsidiaries and parent companies. The only ones given wide currency usually come from the Fair Trade Commission (FTC). Among other things, the FTC ascertained that members of the six top horizontal groupings cover about 20 percent of their financial needs from group institutions, and about 65 percent chose their lead bank from within the group.[5] Another FTC study traced the level of association between the six largest trading companies and their affiliates; the levels were 12 percent for purchases and five percent for sales.[6] While modest, these figures are far from negligible (and it must be recalled that the horizontal groupings are the loosest).

Given the commercial interaction with other members, the reverse obviously applies with regard to outsiders. There are fewer opportunities for unrelated firms to sell to members of horizontal groupings; there is even less room for them to supply parts to the vertical groupings; and they have trouble getting into that portion of the market that is dominated by distribution *keiretsu*. This aspect is less attractive and is therefore glossed over by those who participate in groupings and the government. If anything, they are at great pains to deny any exclusiveness. Still, if there is no advantage to being in a *keiretsu*, why bother?[7]

Notes

1. For details of group membership, see Dodwell Marketing Consultants, *Industrial Groupings in Japan*, Tokyo, biannual, and Toyo Keizai, *Kigyo Keiretsu Soran (Directory of Corporate Links)*, Tokyo, annual.
2. Dodwell, op. cit., 1988/89 edition, pp. 36-37.
3. Fair Trade Commission, *The Fair Trade Commission's Approach to Trade Friction*, Tokyo, April 1983.
4. Dan Fenno Henderson, *Foreign Enterprise in Japan*, (Tokyo: Tuttle, 1975), p. 141.
5. See Fair Trade Commission, *The Present State of Industrial Groups*, Tokyo, June 1983.
6. See Fair Trade Commission, *The Fair Trade Commission's Approach to Trade Friction*, Tokyo, April 1983.
7. For another analysis of the three types of *keiretsu*, see United States International Trade Commission. *Japan's Distribution System and Options for Improving U.S. Access*, June 1990.

7

The Big Eight . . . And More

First, and in many ways foremost, of the various *keiretsu* are the horizontal groupings. Given the key position of the bank, they are also known as banking "alignments" or *kin'yu keiretsu* and also capital *keiretsu*. They are the oldest groups—some tracing their origins back a century or more—and are the largest in terms of capital, sales, and employees. They also have the broadest scope since they include companies pursuing a wide range of activities. Finally, they posses the highest status and greatest political clout.

Three of these groups are extensions of the prewar *zaibatsu*, which were much tighter structures that were owned by wealthy families, controlled by holding companies, and run by managers with an interest in all aspects of their business. The *zaibatsu* played an even more decisive role in prewar economic development than the *keiretsu* since then. Some of this influence was negative, since the *zaibatsu* supported or tolerated the rise of militarism, colonial expansion, and then the war.

The occupation authorities moved to disband the *zaibatsu* as early as 1945. The families were dispossessed, numerous managers purged, groups split up, and even some individual companies divided. Some of the lesser *zaibatsu* disappeared. Mitsubishi, Mitsui, and Sumitomo, however, managed to survive, even if at first they were disjointed. Over the years they restored previous links, and in some cases companies merged back into their original form. After the revisions of the Antimonopoly Act in 1949 and 1953, they could shed any pretense of separateness and even operate under their old names.[1]

Several other groups—somewhat more loosely organized but quite similar in nature—arose through the efforts of influential banks to create their own groupings. These were banks with long histories that could attract old and new customers. They also absorbed parts of the lesser *zaibatsu* that had not reformed on their own. Those that have risen to true *keiretsu* status revolve around the Dai-Ichi Kangyo, Fuji, and Sanwa Banks. The groupings created by the Tokai Bank and Industrial Bank of Japan are weaker.

There are certain differences between the various horizontal groupings. For example, some are considerably larger than others. The biggest in every sense is Mitsubishi, with 160 member companies, almost 31 trillion yen in sales, and 360,000 employees. It is followed closely by Mitsui and Sumitomo, and a bit further off by the Fuji (or Fuyo), DKB, and Sanwa Groups. The Tokai and IBJ Groups are considerably smaller.[2]

A second difference arises with regard to the mix of companies. Some are more industrial, with Mitsubishi placing great stress on heavy industry and Sumitomo on metals. Others are more commercial, such as Mitsui. The bank-related groups tend to have less heavy and more light industry. Yet, with the huge number of members, each group displays impressive versatility, including most services, transport, industrial, financial, and real estate operations. Just how comprehensive and diversified a *keiretsu* can be is shown in Figure 7.1, giving the Mitsui Group as an example.

More important than size in many ways is the degree of coordination. Here, too, the hierarchy runs pretty much along the same lines, with the older and larger units exercising stricter control. Each of these groups has an inner circle of members, about twenty or so, which can function more efficiently. They meet regularly (once a month) through presidents' councils. They discuss matters of common concern and are in a position to make important decisions. Just what the decisions are, and how far the solidarity reaches, is unknown since the proceedings are secret and rarely disclosed.

In addition to such meetings, there is a certain degree of crossholding, which usually takes the form of banks, insurance companies, and trading companies holding shares in industrial and other ventures. But some manufacturers hold shares in one another. Normally, each company has a rather small holding, a few percent or so, but several may join in, and they can end up with 10 percent, 20 percent, or more between them. There are also cases where lesser members are practically the subsidiaries of major ones. The crossholding ratio varies from one group to the next, with a high of 21 percent in the Sumitomo Group and a low of 14 percent in the Sanwa Group.[3]

Figure 7.1
The Mitsui Group

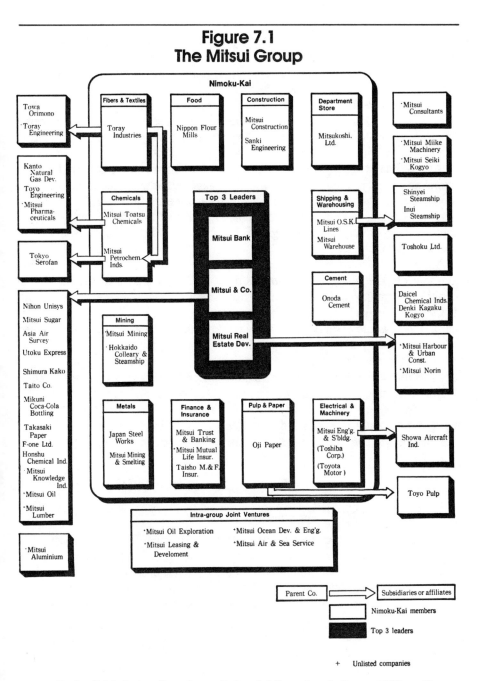

CREDIT: Dodwell Marketing Consultants, *Industrial Groupings in Japan*, 1988, p. 61.

The links are further consolidated by appointing directors to one another's board. Again, it is more likely that the banks, insurance companies, and trading companies will send directors (and auditors) to the manufacturers, and manufacturers will send directors to companies they dominate. A study of the number of directors sent to group companies by key members showed as much as five percent of the total. To this can be added another three percent or so who came from government offices and public corporations. This government connection should not be ignored, either.[4]

As will be noted periodically, while these relations are close, they are far from complete or exclusive. They are much weaker than the relations that existed among the prewar *zaibatsu*, and may be weakening even further. After all, members have relations with many companies that are outside the given grouping. Some adhere loosely to several groupings, and others have shifted from one to another over the years.

Moreover, these companies are all independent entities, albeit with some external control. They have their own boards of directors and managers, their own capital and employees, and they must fulfill their own corporate goals above all. If they were expected to do something that went against this principle, it is not certain they would comply. It is highly unlikely that such a thing would be asked of them by their peers—at least not without adequate compensation.

What is expected of the companies is not absolute dedication to the group's needs, but rather cooperation in their mutual interest and showing preference to their counterparts. This preference can be limited, occasionally even marginal, but it must be real in order to create the sort of solidarity that is necessary to maintain the group. From their continued existence and activities, it can be assumed that the members are willing to meet this relative commitment.

Cooperation Economy-Wide

In each of these groups a decisive role is played by the bank, which is the primary source of finance for the group companies. This function was especially essential in the early period when the *keiretsu* were being formed. In order to reconstruct and expand, companies needed funds they could not generate internally or receive from the government. The importance of the bank has decreased somewhat since then as companies have increased their capitalization, expanded their internal funding, and can now raise money through stocks and bonds. But it has always been wise to remain on good terms with the bank.

The group bank was most often the lead bank of the other members. It was not their sole bank, but the one they turned to first and could be expected to give them privileged treatment. Most companies had another bank, occasionally several other banks, they could fall back on. But they borrowed more heavily from the group bank and thereby promoted its advancement. In return, it was easier for companies to get credit and it was also possible to do so on somewhat better interest and repayment terms.

Insurance companies play a subsidiary role in funding group members, often by purchasing their stock or bonds. In return, group members would give these companies priority when their services were needed. The shipping line would cover its risks, and the traders theirs, to the benefits of the marine insurers. Group members would give the fire, casualty, and life insurance companies priority in the same way. Again, they might also contract insurance elsewhere if the conditions were good enough, but that happened infrequently since they were favored customers.

Second only to the bank in its influence is the trading company or *sogo shosha*. Each group is tied up with one of those. The basic alignment is Mitsubishi with Mitsubishi Corp., Mitsui and Mitsui & Co., DKB with C. Itoh, Fuyo with Marubeni, Sumitomo with Sumitomo Corp., Sanwa with Nissho Iwai, and Tokai with Toyo Menka. Two of the smaller traders—Kanematsu-Gosho and Nichimen—have looser relations with DKB and Sanwa, respectively. By the way, each of these giant traders has its own grouping of hundreds of subsidiaries with the top six alone boasting some 2,431.

As is generally known, these nine *sogo shosha* play a substantial role in Japan's trade. Their combined annual sales amounted to over 98 trillion yen in 1988, a figure that has been rising unevenly but steadily. The ranking has varied somewhat over the years, with the present leader C. Itoh handling nearly 16 trillion yen, while even the smallest, Kanematsu-Gosho, accounted for over 4 trillion. Collectively, the nine loom exceptionally large with 42 percent of all exports and 74 percent of all imports. There is nothing like this in any other economy.

While the stress is often placed on their external activities, it should be noted that these traders actually import more than they export. They are also deeply involved in domestic distribution. In fact, domestic sales represent 47 percent of their total turnover. The products they are most active in include petrochemicals and chemicals, steel and other metals, plant, machinery and construction, foodstuffs, and textiles. In these sectors, and to a lesser extent elsewhere, it is hard not to encounter the *sogo shosha* in one form or another.

One further function is financing. The *sogo shosha* regularly provide credit to the lesser companies they deal with. Domestically, this involves giving local distributors or manufacturers advances or loans. While this makes these companies somewhat more dependent on the trader, it also works in the other direction in that the trader must help them prosper if it is to earn a proper return on its money or, in bad times, avoid defaults. This is another reason why traders are partial to their own network.

Thus, while the *sogo shosha* are in the business of trading, they are not interested in dealing with every possible partner. They would tend not to cooperate with foreign companies that produce competitive goods. They prefer handling bulk commodities to processed ones since this is done locally by their clients. They would even tend not to take on finished products that compete directly with manufacturers whose exports they carry.

Manufacturers are an important part of this system. They often process the raw materials that are imported by the trading companies. As much as possible, they give priority to the *sogo shosha* in their own group. They also give it priority over foreign companies that might wish to sell them the same raw materials directly or in processed form. This precedence was particularly strict during the earlier period, but has since been relaxed somewhat. It has been realized that low-cost raw materials are essential, and more manufacturers are importing directly. Also, the cost of processing certain raw materials, such as bauxite for aluminum, is simply too high.

Manufacturers frequently cooperate with one another. The steel mills will sell much of their output to major users such as shipbuilders and automobile makers, some of which may well be in the group. They also pass it along to fabricators and smaller users. There is some amount of sales between more distant sectors, such as of chemicals to assorted manufacturers, paper to the whole range of firms, or computers to group offices across the board. Here, however, the relations become more tenuous and group membership is helpful but far from decisive.

While most of these transactions are current and ongoing, the groups also launch major projects that draw several of them into a joint company. Such companies have been set up, for example, for leasing, urban development, and information services. Others were mounted for overseas investments, especially in the mining and processing of raw materials.[6] This binds the partners closely together and makes it unlikely that they would seek outside sources.

While one should not exaggerate the effectiveness of these links, it is easy to see their advantages. They offer a foot in the door for any group member and a reasonable reception, something that is precious. They can perhaps clinch a sale even if the price, quality, or other conditions are not the very best but other dealings or group solidarity militate in favor. They may even urge their employees to purchase goods from related companies, as in Sumitomo's "buy Mazda" and "buy Asahi beer" campaigns.[7] When this happens, a company can count on a sales base that outsiders simply do not have.

What about outsiders? Where do they fit? They are not actually excluded from doing business with group members. If they have a special item that is needed and not provided by anyone in the group, they would find ready entry. If they have a product that is not directly competitive, even to those available, they may stand a chance. If their articles are directly competitive, things are more difficult. They can still sell, but they must fight for every sale and try to provide goods that are of even higher quality, at even lower prices, and with quite exceptional delivery and service.

Notes

1. See William W. Lockwood, ed., *The State and Economic Enterprise in Japan*, (Princeton: Princeton University Press, 1965), pp. 195-504.

2. For a description of the major *keiretsu*, see Dodwell, op. cit., pp. 36-137.

3. Dodwell, op. cit., p. 8. The crossholding ratio is defined as the shares held by group companies as a percentage of paid-up capital.

4. Ibid., p. 10.

5. See Kunio Yoshihara, *Sogo Shosha* (Tokyo: Oxford University Press, 1982), and Alexander K. Young, *The Sogo Shosha: Japan's Multinational Trading Companies* (Boulder: Westview, 1979).

6. See Jon Woronoff, *Japan's Commercial Empire*, (Armonk: M.E. Sharpe, 1984).

7. *Japan Economic Almanac 1985*, Japan Economic Journal, April 1985, p. 216.

C H A P T E R

8

Enterprise Groupings

While smaller and less diversified, the vertical groupings are exceedingly effective because they are aligned more strictly on a dominant enterprise, which explains why they are called enterprise (*kigyo*) *keiretsu*. They are also known as production *keiretsu* because they link manufacturers and suppliers. This category is characterized by far greater specialization and closer relations between the various members, which can be translated into enhanced commercial integration of their activities. They form much more of a self-contained unit and strive to be reasonably self-sufficient, an urge that affects the rest of the business community.

Just how many vertical groupings exist is a matter of conjecture, and the number picked will depend mainly on the cutoff point. Dodwell now lists nearly 40 major ones with at least 1 trillion yen in sales.[1] They, too, have large memberships running from 30 to 40 for smaller ones to 200 for Nippon Steel. Among the most comprehensive groupings are those of Toyota and Nissan for automakers, Hitachi and Matsushita for electronics, and Nippon Steel, Japan's largest integrated steelmaker. But there are others that are not so much smaller and many more that follow exactly the same pattern, although they cannot vie in size.

These groupings are vertical in the sense that they handle several links in the production chain. The Nippon Steel Group, for example, has members that are engaged in mining, general steel production, making of ordinary and special steels as well as other metals and ferroalloys, and finally manufacture of metallic products and machinery. Other members are less directly involved but contribute to the basic thrust, such as companies for construction, transportation, and trading.

Both Hitachi and Toshiba, makers of electronics and electrical equipment, cover this range with a series of generalized companies that produce a variety of products and more specialized ones for telecommunications, consumer articles, heating appliances, medical gear, or batteries. They extend into general machinery, transportation machinery, and plant engineering. This is rounded out with makers of wire and cable, chemicals, special steels and tools.

The Matsushita Group is somewhat more focused on consumer electronics, although it has some companies making industrial items. Certain members produce parts while others turn out finished products like audio equipment, televisions and VCRs, refrigerators, or air conditioners. Nissan and Toyota produce a narrower range of finished products. But the variety of parts supplied by members is extensive: engines, transmissions, ventilators, carburetors, gaskets, springs and on and on. This is the pattern not only for the companies mentioned but for just about all electronics and automotive companies. It is shown in some detail for the Matsushita Group in Figure 8.1.

A looser, more varied structure exists for the groups that originally arose from private railway lines and spread in various directions, like Tokyu and Seibu. They have a land transportation unit, including the railway and perhaps bus lines, shipping, and aviation. Then comes real estate and construction due to their landholdings and need to build. But the emphasis has shifted into commerce, with trading and wholesale companies as well as department stores, supermarkets, and other retail outlets. Most recently, these groups added leisure services like recreation, hotels, and travel agencies.

The organization of these groupings, in which the pieces fit together so nicely, is much more constraining than in any of the horizontal groupings. That is primarily because the ownership position of the core or parent company is much stronger. Many of the group members are mere subsidiaries, and in those that enjoy some autonomy the shareholdings are much higher, often 50 percent or more.

This development has come about in three ways. Some companies spun off new firms as their divisions expanded, the path taken largely by Hitachi and Toyota. Others absorbed or bought into going concerns that ran into trouble or needed financial and management assistance. This was more the case for Nissan, although that sort of thing happens throughout the groupings. The third technique was to establish joint ventures with other group members, nongroup members, or foreign companies. In addition to actual group members, there are slews of suppliers and subcontractors who provide mainly parts or services.

The units assimilated in these ways are not small companies but full-fledged groups (and sometimes erstwhile rivals) like Fuji Heavy Industries for Nissan,

Figure 8.1
The Matsushita Group

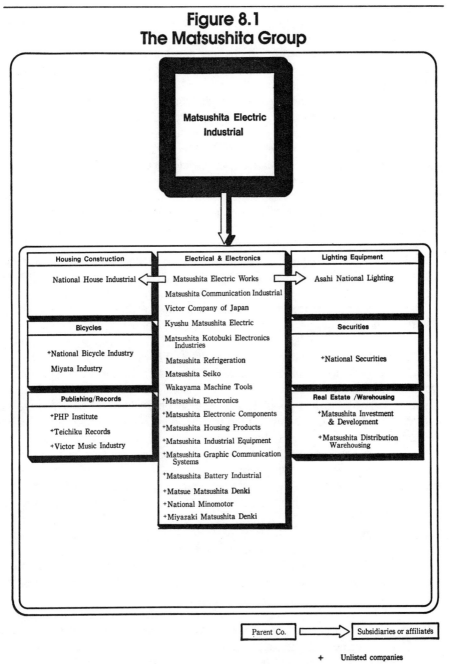

Matsushita Electric Industrial

Housing Construction	Electrical & Electronics	Lighting Equipment
National House Industrial	Matsushita Electric Works	Asahi National Lighting

Electrical & Electronics:
- Matsushita Electric Works
- Matsushita Communication Industrial
- Victor Company of Japan
- Kyushu Matsushita Electric
- Matsushita Kotobuki Electronics Industries
- Matsushita Refrigeration
- Matsushita Seiko
- Wakayama Machine Tools
- +Matsushita Electronics
- +Matsushita Electronic Components
- +Matsushita Housing Products
- +Matsushita Industrial Equipment
- +Matsushita Graphic Communication Systems
- +Matsushita Battery Industrial
- +Matsue Matsushita Denki
- +National Minomotor
- +Miyazaki Matsushita Denki

Bicycles
- +National Bicycle Industry
- Miyata Industry

Publishing/Records
- +PHP Institute
- +Teichiku Records
- +Victor Music Industry

Securities
- +National Securities

Real Estate /Warehousing
- +Matsushita Investment & Development
- +Matsushita Distribution Warehousing

Parent Co.	⇒	Subsidiaries or affiliates

+   Unlisted companies

CREDIT: Dodwell Marketing Consultants, *Industrial Groupings in Japan,* 1988, p. 219.

Hino and Diahatsu for Toyota, and Victor Company for Japan for Matsushita. More impressive is the interlinking of Toshiba and Ishikawajima-Harima Heavy Industries (IHI), itself a leading shipbuilder and maker of machinery and metal products. This was arranged through a crossholding of shares, with Toshiba becoming the major shareholder of IHI.

Naturally, a commanding ownership position was used to exert substantial control over the group members. This could be done through the appointment of directors (and even presidents) and transfer of personnel. It also took the form of presidential councils or more informal clubs of company executives, always under the chairmanship of the group leader. Even stricter in the imposition of rules were the associations created for the suppliers and subcontractors, working them into the production scheme of the assembler.

Nor should it be forgotten that some of these groups are not the bureaucratic units that are supposedly typical of Japan, but groups that were formed by dynamic entrepreneurs and where the founder or his heirs are still active, such as Matsushita, Toyota, Tokyu, and Seibu. There—no matter what the organigrams may show—leadership emanates from one man and his close associates, and there are limited possibilities of evading this further down.

The last factor is commercial. Most of the group members are the suppliers or clients of one another and constantly do business together. In this relationship, it tends to be the client that has the upper hand. The client can impose its will all the more readily to the extent that it is the biggest, and in many cases the sole, buyer. The regulation is most stringent as regards the suppliers' networks in which parts are procured by automotive or electronics makers. It is somewhat less effective where makers of finished goods can offer their products to a broader range of clients. If they have to sell through the trading, wholesale, or retail firms run by the parent company, there is additional pressure.

That this is not theoretical, and that the leverage is very real, can be shown from several examples that are quite close to the norm. Fuji Tekko, a maker of transmission and axle parts, is owned to 34 percent by Nissan and sell 86 percent of its output to Nissan. Nippondenso, an electrical parts maker, is owned to 22 percent by Toyota (and another seven percent by Toyoda Loom) and sells over half its output to Toyota.[2] Even Fuji Heavy Industries, of which Nissan is a shareholder, makes Nissan cars along with its own Subaru. Both Hino and Daihatsu produce large numbers of Toyotas. Many members of the Matsushita family, even though relatively autonomous on paper, still sell through Matsushita Electric Trading and thousands of local shops.[3]

As must be evident, each one of these vertical groupings is a large and powerful unit in its own right. But most of them are also part of, or at least related to, one of the major horizontal groupings. The relations can take some of the forms referred to earlier. The primary relations are financing from the banks and trading through the *sogo shosha*. Thus, Nissan is part of the Fuyo Group, and Toyota sits on both the Mitsui and Tokai Group councils, borrowing largely from those banks. Hitachi is somewhat more independent, dealing with the Fuji, Sanwa, and DKB banks and sitting on the councils of the first two. Nippon Steel sells through Mitsui & Co. and Mitsubishi Corp., as both groups lack a large steel manufacturer.

This linkage enhances the position of both units, horizontal and vertical. It increases the concentration of productive and marketing capabilities and ties even more companies into a broader nexus whose ramifications cannot possibly be overlooked.

Keeping It All in the "Family"

From even the briefest description of this system, it is reasonably clear how it works. It is essentially an institutionalization of the subcontracting networks that exist everywhere, but are usually rather fluid and informal. This time, the units are worked into a hierarchical structure from which the dominant or parent companies procure their necessary parts, materials, and services. This makes for an extremely integrated production machine, which is doubtlessly one of the secrets of Japan's industrial success.

This process is easiest to grasp in the automotive industry. There, the automakers are just assemblers who produce relatively few parts on their own. The bulk of the parts come from a number of primary suppliers that produce engines, electrical parts, drive, transmission, and steering parts, suspension and brake parts, body parts, and accessories. Other companies provide the metal, rubber, glass, plastic, and other basic materials. Both of these sets of suppliers may well be group members, especially the former. How this is done in the Nissan Group is shown in Figure 8.2.

Beneath this are further layers of secondary, tertiary, and lesser subcontractors. Some produce items that go into the parts like springs, screws, forgings, castings, and pressings. Others engage in necessary activities such as plating, painting, welding, and so on. These are usually very small firms, perhaps partly owned by the group members or suppliers—if not, certainly dependent on them.

It is hard to exaggerate how complete this supplier network is since, for all practical purposes, it is capable of supplying just about every part, material, or service the assembler could possibly use. Should there be a gap somewhere, it would not be surprising if the parent company were to set up a new subsidiary. It is impossible to tell what share of the total value of a finished automobile, say, is generated from among group members or subsidiaries, but it is certainly the overwhelming majority.

The other vertical groupings also operate on the same basis to meet their specific needs. The electrical and electronics companies have parts suppliers, many of them captive, a fair number actually group members. The steel and

Figure 8.2
The Nissan Group

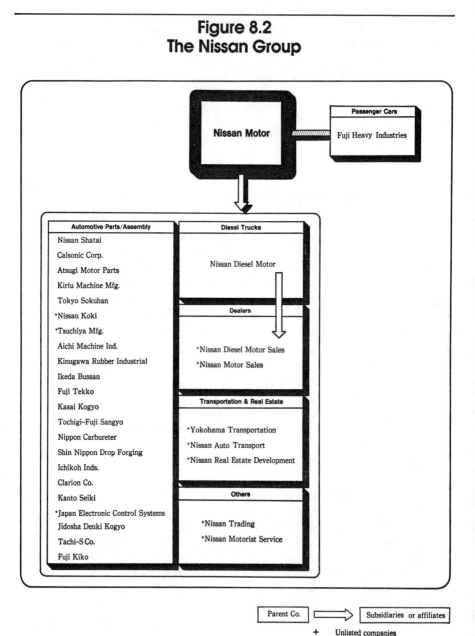

CREDIT: Dodwell Marketing Consultants, *Industrial Groupings in Japan*, 1988, p. 256.

shipbuilding companies are also well endowed with suppliers and, often more important, subcontractors. They will handle such tasks as welding and painting in addition to supplying certain parts.

There is a second advantage to these groups that is particularly adapted to Japanese needs. In a business community where it is common to develop deep and lasting relations, it would be unpleasant if an established client were not able to obtain what it wanted from a traditional supplier. The client might then be forced to go shopping elsewhere, which would be awkward. It would be considerably more disagreeable for the supplier, since it is conceivable that the client might stray. Having purchased one article, the client might notice others and be drawn into a close relationship with a competitor.

Japanese manufacturers, and especially groups, therefore tend to produce just about everything they can in their own line. They want to have the broadest possible range so that there is no need to turn to anyone else. This applies most aptly to the electrical, electronics and automotive industries, but it applies to others as well, such as producers of textiles, chemicals, pharmaceuticals, and even publishers.

This could take the form, for example, of major automobile makers like Toyota and Nissan producing cars of varied size and style to cover much of the market. The gaps are then filled through associates like Daihatsu and Fuji. But it is more pronounced for electrical goods, especially household appliances and consumer electronics. Each one of the top makers produces just about every possible article so that someone entering its store will not have to look elsewhere.

Once again, should there be some gap, the inclination is to fill it from within the group. It would, of course, be feasible to import the item, and this is sometimes done, at least in the initial period. But few articles are so special that they could not be produced by one member or another of the extensive company "family." This is not difficult for a firm like Toyota, say, with 220 primary suppliers and over a thousand secondary and tertiary ones, or Matsushita with over 500 subsidiaries and affiliates.[4]

The integration of the railway-retailing empires like Tokyu and Seibu displays some of these aspects, but in a much less acute form since they are in fields that are not as directly related. True, the travel agency, located in the department store, can sell tickets on the airline or weekends in the hotel. Customers can be encouraged to buy insurance or use credit. And the railway line is a major conveyance to the department store. But this does not add up to much.

Similarly, there has been some diversifications so that a customer can stick to the company. Thus, alongside the original railway line, there are now bus and other transport companies, shipping firms, and airlines. More striking is the knack of these groups, and most major retailers, to assume different forms to get into different market segments and price categories. Both Tokyu and Seibu have not only department stores but supermarkets (known as superstores), convenience or specialty stores, and fast food outlets. This has been done by most of the major retailers, including Daiei, Ito-Yokado, Jusco, and so on.[5]

There is no question about the advantages of the system to the parent company. It is guaranteed, more than could possibly be obtained from independent suppliers, on-time delivery, good quality, and low price. It can make its production plans and sales forecasts known to the suppliers, which can then adjust their own schedules accordingly. Due to the close relations, if it is necessary to introduce a new product, the design and other particulars can be worked out together. If, for any reason, the parent company were in financial difficulty, it could prevail on its suppliers to bear some of the brunt and decrease their prices.[6]

There are also advantages for the suppliers. They can count on a steady stream of orders and will find it easier to plan their future operations. If in difficulty, they may get financial and management assistance. Admittedly, in such a tight situation, it is hard for them to make very big margins, but this would seem to be compensated for by the stability of the relationship. While they may have to compress prices when things are rough, they may be able to get a bit more in boom times. Or, if pressed hard, they can exert some pressure on their own subcontractors.

There is is a definite mood of "all in the same boat" in these arrangements. Some of it comes from the human connections, since subsidiaries often have directors who have been appointed to them and other personnel who may have retired there. They will naturally maintain their allegiance to the parent company, but also look out for their new colleagues. Some also comes from the financial connections. As a shareholder, often a major one, it would be foolish to hurt profits that one subsequently receives as dividends.

Where does this leave outsiders? In a disadvantageous position, to say the least. It is difficult to make sales because the whole system is so closely integrated and there are almost no gaps. Just about anything a parent company, assembler, or retailer might want can be made by another company it is related to in one way or another. Only in very special cases—where an exceptional new product is launched or the producer has proprietary rights—is it necessary to turn to an outsider.

Notes

1. For a description of the major vertical groupings, see Dodwell, op. cit.
2. See Dodwell, *The Structure of the Japanese Auto Parts Industry* (Tokyo, 1983), pp. 139-275.
3. See Dodwell, *Key Players in the Japanese Electronics Industry* (Tokyo, 1985).
4. Ibid.

5. See Dodwell, *The Structure of the Japanese Retail and Distribution Industry* (Tokyo, 1985).

6. *Far Eastern Economic Review*, June 21, 1990, p. 54.

C H A P T E R
9

From Manufacturing
to Marketing

The third category of groupings is less known but no less effective for that. It is the distribution *keiretsu* (*ryutsu keiretsu*), also translated as "distribution channeling arrangements" and "integrated marketing networks." Smaller, less capitalized, and less visible, they have the tremendous advantage of being closest to the final consumer. That is where their real power comes from and why anyone doing business with Japan would be most unwise to dismiss them.

The distribution *keiretsu* strictly speaking consist of groupings in which the manufacturer controls or dominates the marketing channels for its products, often down to the last detail. It may set up its own wholesale operations and sell to other secondary or tertiary wholesalers. Or it may reach further to the retail outlets, which it sometimes owns, sometimes merely manipulates.[1]

The derivation of these groupings is partly historical. Some sectors were new to Japan when they arose in prewar days or were resumed after the war, and there were not enough wholesalers or retailers to handle them. In order to sell the goods, the makers had no choice but to create their own marketing machinery, their own wholesaling operations, and sometimes even the local dealerships or neighborhood strores that carried the goods. This occurred for household appliances, sewing machines, consumer electronics, automobiles, motorcycles, and Western musical instruments.

In other sectors, it was the importer that branched into production. Realizing that the goods could be produced as well, as cheaply, and more conveniently in Japan—while giving the entrepreneur a healthy value added—wholesalers either set up their own companies or entrusted related companies with the task. In some cases, these were joint ventures with foreign companies that possessed the know-how. This path was taken most notably in sporting goods and pharmaceuticals, with production quickly overtaking marketing as the pivot.

The other reasons were similar to those that moved businesses to create groupings in all other sectors, such as loyalty and stability of the relationship. By controlling the outlets, it was easier to be certain that sales would be undertaken actively and that the wholesaler or retailer would not readily switch to another maker. For this, it was necessary to make the marketing channels do the producer's bidding rather than the other way around.

Control was imposed by means that should be familiar by now. The producer held shares in the wholesaler, when it was not a wholly-owned subsidiary, and sometimes also in the retailers, although less frequently and less extensively. For historical reasons, it might also occur that the wholesaler held stock in the producer. This shareholding enabled the lead company to impose directors on the sales outlets and, in some instances even more important, to have someone sitting in the committees that decided just which products to carry and how hard to push them.

Although not at quite as high a level, there was a further practice whose benefits can hardly be overlooked. Manufactures would occasionally "lend" their personnel to the retailers. These were usually junior employees who thereby gained contact with the public and learned about the trade. More important, of course, was that they appeared wearing the company uniform or badge and encouraged customers to buy company products. This was often done with even more zeal than by the proprietor of the outlet who, not wishing to upset the supplier and habitually short-staffed, went along with the exercise.

In other cases, where there was no actual ownership, wholesale outlets might become financially dependent on the manufacturer due to the need for credit.[2] The situation of most retailers was even more delicate since they always had a skimpy cash flow and easily became dependent on rebates. Providing credit was not only a necessary task; it was done specifically to create such a state of dependence, which permitted the manufacturers or wholesalers to impose their will on the retailers.

As mentioned, this sort of relationship arose especially in certain sectors, including automobiles and motorcycles, household appliances and consumer electronics, optical goods (eyeglasses, cameras), pharmaceuticals, cosmetics, sewing machines, and alcoholic beverages. It also emerged for musical instruments, sporting goods, and even foodstuffs. Companies that use the technique extensively include such well-known names as Matsushita (and most other electronics makers), Nissan, Toyota (and their rivals), Shiseido (and other cosmetics firms), Suntory (and other brewers and distillers), K. Hattori (for Seiko watches), Nippon Gakki (electones, pianos, and other instruments), and Hoya (eyeglasses).

However, makers of other articles that are not normally sold directly to the final consumer were forced to do so by another quirk of the distribution system. Department stores, and even supermarkets to some extent, rent out stalls or floor space to manufactures, which are expected to decorate, staff, and supply them with goods. Makers therefore have to go into marketing even if the overall establishment is not theirs. Articles frequently sold this way include cosmetics and fashion goods, household furnishings and furniture, and foreign and domestic foods.

While they are not truly distribution *keiretsu*, there are other arrangements that sometimes use similar techniques and end up with roughly the same results. These are relationships in which it is the marketing unit that controls the producers. Since that unit may be not just one or two distributors but a whole family of retailers, it can be exceedingly effective. A good example of this are the Tokyu and Seibu Retail Groups. This composition of the latter is given in Figure 9.1.

Another variation occurs with the *sogo shosha*. Their main activity is to import commodities and raw materials in bulk. But they do not always sell them directly. In order to simplify their task and acquire the necessary expertise, they tend to create separate wholesalers for different product lines. Some of those working with the big nine deal in special steels and other metals, petroleum and gas, chemicals, textiles, plant and equipment, or foodstuffs.

The trading companies also go a big step further by setting up or joining with other firms that process their bulk imports. Just a few among the many ventures undertaken by the nine top traders include making of steel sheet, wire, pipe, etc., plastic products, timber, fertilizer, and so on. They are most active in foodstuffs. Such units produce edible oils, frozen fish and meat, soft drinks, and refined sugar.

Wholesalers, whether independent or integrated into the general trading companies, also engage in such production activities. As noted, the pharmaceutical wholesalers were so ambitious that they eventually turned into manufacturers. Others have done the same for their own product lines, whether chemicals, foodstuffs, sporting goods, or toys.

Finally, and most recently, the major department and chain stores have taken to selling more products under their own brand. This is being done by Tokyu and Seibu, and even more aggressively by Daiei and Ito-Yokado. Smaller chains are also joining in. The articles include especially clothing, household goods, and foodstuffs. Private brand sales already amount to about a tenth of total turnover.

Figure 9.1
The Seibu Retail Group

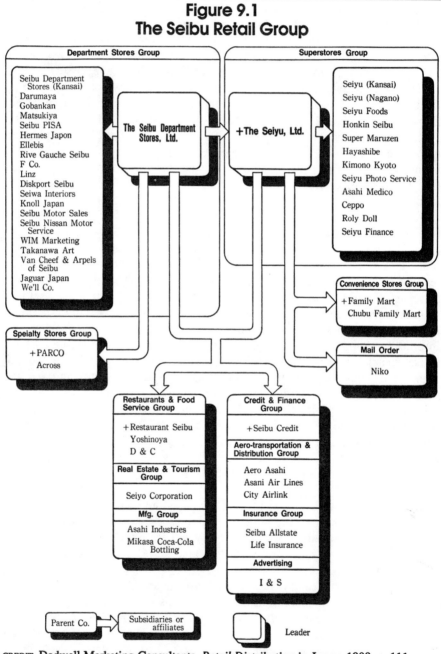

CREDIT: Dodwell Marketing Consultants, *Retail Distribution in Japan*, 1988, p. 111.

At first products were made by existing manufacturers, but the retailers have been increasingly setting up their own operations.

In these setups, the shareholding is much higher than it is for horizontal groupings or distribution *keiretsu*. Most are well over 50 percent, and 100 percent ownership seems to be the goal, one that is frequently attained. From such a position it is easy to exercise control as regards not only appointment of directors but also the whole staff. This influence penetrates all aspects of the subsidiaries' activities.

Whatever the type of arrangement, the relationship between manufacturers and distributors is uncommonly close in Japan. Indeed, as pointed out by Mark Zimmerman, a long-time businessman and former president of the American Chamber of Commerce in Japan, the distribution network is actually "an extension of the company itself." As he indicates: "Senior executives are obligated to visit each distributor at least once a year to reaffirm their commitment. Similarly, the distributor will visit the head office, rest houses, factories, and branches of the Japanese company, knowing that he will be treated like an honored family member."[3]

The other side of this close relationship is that little room remains for newcomers, local or foreign. As Zimmerman notes: "The existing distribution network is restricted to current manufacturers, and it is unlikely to be susceptible to an offer to switch to a new, untried manufacturer. Building a distribution network from scratch can take many years, which is one of the main reasons why foreign companies have trouble expanding in Japan unless they can piggyback on the already existing network of a joint-venture partner."[4]

Dominating Distribution

The motives for establishing these groupings have already been described by echoing the standard Japanese allusions to stability and loyalty. These are, indeed, fine virtues. But they can be more than that. They can be excellent commercial principles that redound to the credit of the dominant party. It only takes some simple illustrations to show this.

Loyalty means, among other things, that the wholesalers and retailers will continue selling the manufacturer's goods year after year. It also implies that, as part of the "family," they will do their best to sell effectively. They will cultivate the clientele, look after its needs, provide efficient service. They will probably throw themselves even more wholeheartedly into the exercise if, as is the underlying aim, they accept exclusivity. Most of the wholesalers and retailers concerned are either bound by contract as sole agents or simply tend to sell only one maker's products for financial or sentimental reasons.

This also makes it easier to accomplish some subsidiary aims of the manufacturer. For example, it is possible for the manufacturer to create a uniform image by imposing its publicity, POS gadgets, mottoes and slogans, and even shop and shelf layout. It can also obtain better feedback since the retailers are more likely to indicate which products do well or poorly, how they can be improved to satisfy the customers, what articles are missing, and so on. The feedback could hardly be more direct than when it passes through sales help loaned to the retailer.

There is a final element, one that is not as noble but certainly plays a crucial role: price. By controlling much of the wholesale and retail network, it is possible to impose fixed prices at which the goods must be sold. Under most contracts, retailers cannot pass goods along to third parties, which might then lower the price, nor would they find it wise to discount goods themselves if warned not to. Resale-price maintenance helps the manufacturer most as it boosts profits. That it may reduce sales is a problem for the retailer.[5]

These are more than ample causes for manufacturers to set up or preserve their own marketing channels. It would seem that the motives of the trading companies, wholesalers, or retailers that establish production operations would be considerably different. In one way they are, in that they seek advantages similar to those of vertical groupings, which want reliable flows of quality products at cheap prices. If they cannot obtain this, they would have been just as well off using established companies.

But as the major or sole owner of manufacturers, they cannot help working in the latters' interest as well. They must make every effort to sell goods or their subsidiaries will be stuck with excess stock or capacity. They must see that the margins are reasonable or they cannot pay personnel and other costs and still have a profit, part of which they collect. They can hardly escape noting that when they sell their own brand goods, as opposed to those of outside suppliers, they not only earn a commission but dividends as well.

One essential dimension of these groupings has been neglected; until it is adequately fathomed, much of the discussion is meaningless. For if the manufacturers had only modest numbers of outlets amidst vast numbers of retailers or dealers who sold the products of several makers—or, quite simply, any maker that offered a proper commission—this phenomenon could be regarded as secondary. That the situation is the complete opposite elevates it to exceptional prominence.

In those sectors where distribution *keiretsu* appear, the vast majority of the outlets might be tied up with one maker or another. This happens for automobiles, motorcycles, cosmetics, eyeglasses, watches, household appliances, consumer electronics, and other articles. In these sectors, it is the exception to encounter a choice of brands. When that exists, the choice may only be in appearance with others just filling out the range of the principle maker with items that are much cheaper, more expensive, or somehow different.

To get an idea of the dimensions involved, it should be stressed that the vast majority of household appliance and electronics stores belong to the leading *keiretsu*. Matsushita has some 27,000, Toshiba 14,000, Hitachi 12,000, Sanyo

6,000, Mitsubishi 5,500, Sharp 5,800 and so on.[6] Very few stores sell foreign products. The situation for automobiles is similar. Toyota has over 4,200 sales units, Nissan and the others proportionately less. Only a few hundred dealers handle imported cars.[7] The same thing happens for motorcycles, where Honda, Yamaha, and Suzuki control most of the outlets, or for eyeglasses with Hoya and watches with Seiko.

Given the role of small retail outlets and the tendency of many Japanese to shop locally, it is decisive for a manufacturer to have an extensive and dense network. If it is not in a given neighborhood, it is entirely possible that it will not sell goods there. Indeed, there is a close correlation between the number of outlets and market share. Using the electronics industry as an example, Matsushita is the top producer with Sony much further down, doubtlessly a function of their marketing machinery in part.

For the third time, it is necessary to consider the position of the outsider. Here, the disadvantages can be even more telling since, if it cannot reach the end consumer, it is hard to sell no matter how good, cheap, or desirable the products.

The first stumbling block arises with the trading companies and the wholesalers, which are widely regarded as the principal gateways to the Japanese market. If one of these companies produces competing goods or has close relations with a manufacturer that does, it is naturally less interested in taking up the goods of outsiders. The situation is still more congenial with chain stores, since their own production is rather limited. But, in all cases, it is most likely that they will gradually be filling their own needs where those needs are largest and most regular, leaving only lesser niches open.

The chances for entry are even more restricted with the distribution *keiretsu*. They were designed specifically to sell the manufacturer's goods and not those of its competitors. Retailers that have been lined up would not break this compact unless there were very tempting advantages. Given the large number of captive outlets, the remainder offer only limited access to the market. And even many supposedly independent retailers are actually tied up with the main domestic manufacturers.[8]

Notes

1. See Dodwell, *The Structure of the Japanese Retail and Distribution Industry* (Tokyo, 1985).
2. Mark Zimmerman, op. cit., p. 137.
3. Ibid., p. 138.
4. Ibid., p. 139.
5. See J. Amanda Covey, "Vertical Restraints under Japanese Law," *Law in Japan*, Vol. 14, 1981, pp. 49-81, and Hideto Ishida, "Anticompetitive Prac-

tices in the Distribution of Goods and Services in Japan: The Problems of the Distribution Keiretsu," *Journal of Japanese Studies*, Vol. 9, No. 2, Summer 1983, pp. 319-34.

6. *The Economist*, September 9, 1989, p. 28.

7. On the situation in the automobile sector, see USITC, op. cit., pp. 58-61.

8. *Financial Times*, September 12, 1989, p. 35.

CHAPTER

10

Living with the System

No matter how much the Japanese government protests that its market is open and businesses deny that their arrangements obstruct trade, it is obvious that the existence of numerous groupings is a barrier of sorts.[1] Even when it is not an absolute barrier, it creates restraints and constricts the room for maneuver. This is done not only for a few products but for a broad spectrum: from raw materials and capital goods to manufactures and quite ordinary consumer articles. It can happen at the level of importers and wholesalers, manufacturers, and distributors. And it involves most of the major players.

It therefore seems justified that foreign governments should ask Japan to reduce the disadvantages and gradually do away with the system. Admittedly, such demands will be hard to enforce in the absence of generally agreed-on international rules and the argument that this is a cultural matter rather than a legal or commercial one (although these links were not as extensive before the war and sometimes violate Japan's own antitrust rules). That probably explains why *keiretsu* were taken up within the Structural Impediments Initiative (SII).

But not much was achieved under the SII. Nor can much progress be expected from foreign pressure (*gaiatsu*). So, the only hope is that change may come about spontaneously within the business community and state. Fortunately, there are some signs that the links are being modified or relaxed.

One of these developments is the tendency of members of the horizontal group-ings, the formidable *keiretsu*, to go their own way more and more. The two core companies in most cases are the bank and the *sogo shosha*. Banks, while always useful, have become less crucial over the years. There are other sources of funds. The trading companies have also slipped somewhat. Bulk commodities, in which they specialize, are less essential and they have not done as well in handling smaller lots of finished products.

This relaxation can be seen in various ways. Member companies now turn more to other banks, including foreign ones. They also export their own products and sometimes import raw materials directly. The crossholding has tended to fall in the major groups, although only slightly so far. Meetings of presidents are regarded as somewhat ritualistic and have less impact on day-to-day operations. Aside from some new sectors, not many joint projects are being launched. And members are buying products outside the group more frequently if they are sub-stantially better or cheaper. This is hardly fatal for the *keiretsu*, but it does leave more openings for outsiders.

Unfortunately, relations within the vertical groupings have become more in-tense than ever. With the harsh economic climate, more and more suppliers and subcontractors, including some that were relatively independent, have turned to the parent companies for financial or management assistance. In order to survive in an increasingly competitive market, the parent companies have also imposed stricter control on quality, delivery, and price. Meanwhile, innovations like com-puterization and robotization make it easier to know just what the lesser members are doing and work them more deeply into the team.

The situation for the distribution *keiretsu* is mixed. On the one hand, the parent companies have sometimes reinforced the integration of retailers by acquiring more of their stock or offering more credit. Some that might otherwise have failed were bought up. Yet, this has become such a heavy burden that certain groups are gradually withdrawing and urging their dealers to be more independent. They are also allowing them to sell products of other makers on occasion. At the same time, in some sectors there has been an increase in the number of independent stores that sell a variety of brands, some of which have become remarkably successful by combining the broader choice with lower prices or better terms.

At this point, it is necessary to consider a very different kind of influence. This is exerted by the Fair Trade Commission, which is Japan's antitrust agency. Established under the Antimonopoly Act of 1947, it has had its share of vicissi-tudes. During the boom years of the 1950s and 1960s, it was weakened by various revisions and government policies. With the recession, however, it was strength-ened by a new revision in 1977. Presently, acting under that mandate, it has been moderately vigorous in enforcing the rules.

The FTC's interests do not coincide with those of foreign companies or gov-ernments, but some of its actions are useful. It has to prevent collusion between firms that could cause unwarranted price hikes and to avoid excessive concentration of sales resulting in monopoly or oligopoly. It therefore opposed any price fixing of domestic or imported goods. It has passed legislation or adopted guidelines to limit the shareholding of banks in all other companies, including group companies. It also limited, albeit at somewhat higher levels, the shareholding of manufacturers in rival firms.[2] This has loosened the groups a bit.

While it cannot intervene in dealings between group members in ordinary circumstances, the FTC definitely has to act when cartels are formed. This includes not only sales cartels, which existed most notoriously for the purchase of soda ash, but also, in varying degrees, imports of pulp and paper, aluminum ingots, petroleum, and so on. Prevention of such collusion and dissolution of the cartels are certainly to the good of foreign companies. But they were upset by its attack on sole agency agreements.[3]

The FTC's primary concerns with distribution *keiretsu* are price-maintenance arrangements and the abuse of rebates to tie-in retailers. Putting an end to both practices would certainly loosen the relationship. This could be a decisive step if it were followed up, as has sometimes been hinted, by an energetic effort to restore independence to the retailers and dealers. No longer bound by law or by debt to their parent company or one large manufacturer, outlets could begin selling the products of several manufacturers. This would be a real breakthrough for foreign products of household appliances, electronics and automobiles among others.

Just how far the Fair Trade Commission will go is uncertain, and many of these promises may not be fulfilled. After all, as noted, the FTC's interests do not necessarily coincide with those of foreign exporters or manufacturers, and it has carefully refrained from doing anything that could be interpreted as playing into the hands of foreigners. Not only that, it has issued various studies of the Japanese market that conclude that it is "open" and "not unfair."[4] That these studies were often vitiated by too narrow a focus or systematic neglect of contrary evidence shows its limits.

Even more significantly, the FTC is not much of a watchdog. It is not a very large or dynamic agency. Its budget and staff are only half that of its American counterpart, and it is heavily dependent on other bodies from which it derives staff and even its director. It is much weaker than the Ministry of International Trade and Industry or Ministry of Finance, which often collude in cooperative business arrangements. It has complained about MITI's antirecession cartels, but its action even against clear violations of antitrust law has been meek, launching many investigations but bringing few suits and imposing only admonitions or minor fines.[5]

So, while these developments are encouraging, it is premature to regard this as the dusk of the *keiretsu*. These groupings are still very large and powerful economically. Their share of capital, sales, labor force, etc., is preponderant and, in some cases, still growing. For example, the *sogo shosha* now handle a larger percentage of imports than before. Personal and financial links have not really weakened, and crossholding remains high, higher even then some decades back.[6] When banks sold shares at the behest of the FTC, they were just bought up by other group members.

Nor is there much chance of the *keiretsu* being contained by political action of the people, who seem to accept them quite tamely, or the government of the ruling Liberal Democratic Party (LDP). In addition to economic might, big business has tremendous political clout through its lobby, the Japan Federation of Economic Organizations (Keidanren). After all, Keidanren is by far the biggest financial contributor to the LDP, and it strongly influences policy-making. Most LDP politicians endorse whatever measures it favors and oppose those it dislikes. Most bureaucrats also support the large companies, which often employ them after retirement, and thus the ministries are equally uninterested in trust-busting or the like.[7]

Fitting In

If *keiretsu,* groupings and intercompany links are not likely to disappear or even weaken noticeably in the near future, it serves little purpose for foreign businessmen to make believe they do not exist, complain about them, or blame failure to penetrate the market on their existence. This may be comforting, but it does not really help. The only approach that makes commercial sense is to figure out how to live with the system.

The first step, one that amazingly few outsiders seem to realize, is quite simply to recognize that groupings and links do exist even if there is nothing similar in their home country. The worst offenders are the Americans, since *keiretsu* would run counter to antitrust laws. Germans, French, and Italians find them more familiar. But, whether foreigners are aware of them or not, the Japanese cannot forget about them for a moment. When he negotiates, as Mark Zimmerman pointed out,

> The questions revolving in the mind of a Japanese contemplating a deal are how the industrial group with which he is affiliated will view the new arrangement with a foreign company; what the association of his industry will have to say; and whether he will be taking unfair advantage, thus causing his competitors to react violently. In fact, the Japanese is as concerned with the impact of the agreement on his standing within the Japanese business community as he is with the direct monetary benefits that his firm will derive from the arrangements.[8]

The second step is to realize that the groupings and links actually make a difference to the foreign company's chances of success. This much has been conceded by businessmen who have been around for a while, but it is often overlooked by newcomers. They think that if they provide adequate quality, decent service, and cheaper prices, they can get in no matter what. It will take time for them to understand that traditional relations and practices can supercede such factors and make things turn out quite differently than expected. That is why frequent references to the actual or potential impact will be made in later sections.

For a start, however, there is no harm in mentioning some of the more blatant examples. Foreign makers of household appliances, watches, cosmetics, etc., soon found that most local stores would not handle their goods, nor could automakers sell through existing dealerships. They had to seek alternative channels. More subtly, exporters who picked the wrong importer found their sales to be very disappointing, and Korean steelmakers could not even sell initially because the traders (related to local producers) just refused to buy. Parts suppliers faced exceptional difficulties in replacing or supplementing existing vendors. Why? Let Edmund J. Reilly, president of Digital Equipment Corporation, Japan explain:

> . . . if a Japanese tire manufacturer goes to the U.S. to sell tires, it can call on automobile manufacturers and if it happens to produce a tire of lower price or higher quality, then it'll make significant inroads relatively quickly. The American automobile company would find it very difficult to say no. There's a system in the U.S. that encourages open bidding and discourages the need for close relationships. It's business.

> Turn that around and say it's an American tire company coming to Japan. Even if that tire happens to be of better quality, lower price, or has a unique strength, it still would be much more difficult because of the relationship that has been built up between the Japanese automobile company and the Japanese tire manufacturer. That relationship plays a much more important role in Japan than it does in the States.[9]

The third step is therefore to study the players and their mutual links very carefully. It is essential to know just which Japanese companies are related to which others, what the actual relationships are, and to what extent they affect the ability to cooperate with foreign companies. Part of this can be obtained from the Dodwell publications or Toyo Keizai Directory; another part must be sought through further, specific research. It would be very foolish not to do this before even contacting a potential Japanese partner, let alone entering into a business arrangement with one.

The fourth step is to figure out where one fits in. It is necessary to decide whether to throw in one's lot with a major grouping or stand aside, trying to cooperate with several or none. If the conclusion is that it is wise to tie up with an existing group, then it is necessary to determine which one. For the moment, only the basic situation and possibilities will be discussed. Further on, there will be more details of the alternatives and practical examples of which routes were taken by various foreign companies.

If a foreign company ties up with a member of a *keiretsu*, be it a trader, manufacturer or bank, this will doubtlessly facilitate access to other group members. It may indeed gain privileged access to a broad circle of companies which can become its customers (and perhaps also distributors, suppliers, or financiers). But, having tied up with one, it may face greater resistance than otherwise from other segments of the business community, whether other groupings or independent companies. Staying outside means that it will not be particularly easy to approach any other companies, but it will also mean that there are no handicaps in trying them all.

Of course, before entering into a close relationship with a given grouping, you have to study meticulously just what other members do. It is best to pick one where there are no direct rivals because, if there are, you may be faced with competing products or find it hard, if not impossible, to reach an agreement. It is, therefore, necessary to look for gaps or niches in the product line and try to fill them. That may imply either joining with a smaller or more incomplete grouping or one that is biased toward other sectors.

As for the specific company with which one does business (whether part of a grouping or not), it is essential to decide whether to cooperate with one that is already specialized in the same sector and knows all about it or not. The former is in a better position to help. But it is also a potential rival. Other companies may be less experienced and helpful, but pose less of a potential threat.

For smaller companies, it may be just as well to keep out of any grouping because they would simply not be taken seriously as a partner. Larger ones, on the other hand, must decide whether to maintain a degree of independence by diversifying, namely entering into relations with companies in several *keiretsu* or sticking to one in which they can be integrated more fully. While this has not happened often, there are some foreign companies whose links are notable, such as Bayer with Sumitomo, BASF with Fuyo, and Philips with Matsushita.[10]

Notes

1. See Senjuro Takahashi, "Is the Distribution System a Trade Barrier?," *Economic Eye*, June 1983, pp. 19-24.
2. The limits are 10 percent (and later five percent) in the former case and 50 percent in the latter.
3. *Financial Times*, January 25, 1990, p. 5.
4. See Fair Trade Commission, *The Fair Trade Commission's Approach to Trade Friction*, April 1983.
5. "Japan Focuses on Its Antitrust Practices," *Wall Street Journal*, November 20, 1989. See also USITC, op. cit., pp. 64-68.
6. According to the FTC, mutual shareholdings of the Mitsubishi, Mitsui and Sumitomo groups accounted for 13 percent of all shares in 1955, 26 percent in 1970 and 32 percent in 1981.
7. See Karel van Wolferen, *The Enigma of Japanese Power* (New York: Vintage Books, 1989), and Jon Woronoff, *Politics, The Japanese Way* (London: Macmillan, and New York: St. Martin's, 1988).
8. Mark Zimmerman, *How to Do Business With The Japanese* (New York: Random House, 1985), pp. 100-101.
9. *Look Japan*, December 1989, p. 13.
10. Dodwell, *Industrial Groupings in Japan*, pp. 280-99.

III

The Distribution Maze

C H A P T E R

11

Distribution as a
Market Factor

In addition to the cultural and business impact of the *keiretsu*, it is the distribution system in general that has led to many non-tariff barrier accusations against Japan, and is perceived by a number of analysts and many business executives to be Japan's primary barrier to imports.[1] Given the fact that Japan's distribution system accounts for 15 percent of overall domestic production and about 18 percent of the total work force,[2] its performance is watched quite closely both within and outside of Japan.

Western observers frequently refer to Japan's traditional distribution system as "mysterious, complex, archaic, old fashioned, stubborn, inefficient and anachronistic."[3] Often, however, the Japanese distribution system continues to be perceived today as it was 20 years ago. As is frequently the case in politics, anecdotal evidence appears to possess a particularly long life span, often exceeding by far the factual circumstances. Yet, a recent report by the U.S. Advisory Committee for Trade Policy and Negotiations (ACTPN) highlights that the "complex, inefficient distribution system" of Japan is a major invisible barrier to trade.[4]

In presenting a current view of the Japanese distribution system, this section aims to accomplish three major objectives. First, it will describe the Japanese distribution system, with a particular focus on consumer products. It will discuss the structure of Japanese distribution channels, highlight unique characteristics of the distribution process, and show how historical factors contributed to this uniqueness. Second, an overview of the current innovations and changes taking place in the distribution system is presented. Third, conclusions will be drawn about the meaning and the impact of these changes to business executives and policymakers.

In approaching these objectives, particular attention is paid to comparing the Japanese and U.S. systems of distribution. Major emphasis also rests on assessing the importation of consumer products into Japan, and on ways to increase the success of such products.

Various limitations and constraints of this section should be called to the attention of the reader. When considering the breadth of import relations of a nation (as outlined in Figure 11.1), four major playing fields exist. These are the exporting country under study, the transfer process of exports, the importing country, and third countries that are exposed to repercussions. Within each of these areas, due to different concerns, a segmentation along type of import is possible, with a grouping into commodities, industrial goods, consumer products, and services representing a rough but adequate generalization. Subsequently, for each area and each type of import, a differentiation between private and public sector activities is needed that can in turn be subdivided into import (export) inhibiting or encouraging. Each one of these subdivisions then raises issues such as financing, distribution, research, and so forth.

Given this framework of necessary areas for a complete study of export (import) relations between two countries, and the fact that these trade relations are only a subset of foreign relations in general, the reader must be aware that this section addresses mainly the area of consumer products within Japan, with a major focus on private and public sector activity in the field of distribution. In this context, it must be remembered that consumer products comprise only a small portion of Japanese imports (see Table 11.1). For example, even though the value of U.S. consumer product exports to Japan has been increasing, in 1988 these products represented only 7 percent of U.S. exports to Japan. In the early 1980s, the major U.S.-Japanese trade frictions and negotiations focused on commodities and industrial products, with services gradually emerging as an additional important issue. Over time, however, it has been argued that more attention needs to be focused on increasing exports of U.S. consumer products to Japan, particularly since "consumer goods exporters [to Japan] experience the greatest frustration because of their exposure to different layers of the [distribution] system."[5]

A second major caveat for the reader is the fact that this work represents the findings of a limited-scale, exploratory study. In addition to the customary (and extensive) literature review, the findings presented here are the result of facts and opinions gathered from policymakers and business executives in both the United

Figure 11.1
Framework for the Study of Trade Relations Between Nations

IMPORT TYPE	CONSUMER PRODUCTS	INDUSTRIAL PRODUCTS	COMMODITIES	SERVICES
Locus of Issue				
Exporting Country	Public Sector obstacles + encouragements			
	Private Sector obstacles + encouragements			
Transfer	Public Sector obstacles + encouragements			
	Private Sector obstacles + encouragements			
Importing Country	Public Sector obstacles + encouragements			
	Private Sector obstacles + encouragements, distribution, financing			
Third Country Repercussions	Public Sector obstacles + encouragements			
	Private Sector obstacles + encouragements			

States and Japan and of personal trade policy experience. The focus here excluded some participants in the Japan distribution system—for example, manufacturers or the famed *sogo shosha,* and the method of analysis focuses primarily on qualitative rather than quantitative data. The scope, however, is sufficiently in-depth to permit for the presentation of some important insights into the Japanese distribution system.

Table 11.1
Japan's Overall Imports and Imports of Consumer Products
(Billion dollars)

Total Imports

	1985	1986	1987	1988
Total imports	129.5	126.4	149.5	187.4
From:	(-5.1)	(-2.4)	(18.3)	(25.3)
U.S.A.	25.8	29.1	31.5	42.0
	(-5.1)	(12.6)	(8.4)	(33.5)
EC	8.9	14.0	17.7	24.1
	(-4.7)	(50.5)	(26.3)	(36.2)
NIEs	9.3	12.4	18.8	33.9
	(-0.3)	(34.2)	(51.1)	(80.3)

Import of Consumer Goods

	1985	1986	1987	1988
Total imports	6.3	9.3	15.7	22.6
From:	(6.0)	(47.9)	(68.5)	(44.3)
U.S.A.	0.9	1.1	1.9	2.9
	(-7.3)	(26.3)	(70.0)	(49.8)
EC	1.8	3.0	5.0	7.3
	(14.7)	(65.6)	(67.2)	(45.7)
NIEs	2.2	3.3	5.8	8.7
	(2.2)	(52.8)	(74.6)	(50.2)

SOURCE: Customs clearance statistics of Japan.

Notes

1. Raymond J. Ahern, "Market Access in Japan: The U.S. Experience," *Congressional Research Service, Report No. 85-37E,* February 14, 1985.

2. Takahide Shiotani, "Outline of Japanese Distribution System," *Business Japan,* August 1988; pp. 89-94.

3. Mitsuaki Shimaguchi and William Lazer, "Japanese Distribution Channels: Invisible Barriers to Market Entry," *MSU Business Topics,* Vol. 27, No. 1; Winter 1979, p. 51.

4. *Analysis of the U.S.–Japan Trade Problem,* Report of the Advisory Committee for Trade Policy and Negotiations, Washington, D.C., February 1989; pp. 11–12.

5. "Strategies for Alleviating Recurrent Bilateral Trade Problems between Japan and the United States, " in *The Japanese Non-Tariff Trade Barriers Issue: American View and Implications for Japan–U.S. Trade Relations,* Report to the Japanese National Institute for Research Advancement, Arthur D. Little, Inc., May 1979; pp. 4–52.

C H A P T E R

12

A Brief Historical Review

Most studies of the Japanese market that deal with the importation of products make extensive reference to the country's complex and unique distribution system. They frequently mention the multilayered channel structure and the fact that wholesalers (or *tonya*) keep on selling to each other, and they highlight the atomistic competition among retailers. As one report notes, Japan has a vast distribution network "with more wholesalers and retailers per capita than any other of the advanced industrial nations."[1] Another study finds that "the manner in which the Japanese channels of distribution are structured and managed presents one of the major reasons for the apparent failure of foreign firms to establish major market participation in Japan."[2] A 1990 report by the U.S. International Trade Commission (USITC) states that "the end result of the close, sometimes overlapping relations and practices in Japan's distribution chains is that it may be unusually difficult and expensive for foreigners, including U.S. exporters, to break into the system."[3]

It needs to be kept in mind, however, that distribution systems usually develop in a certain way for a logical reason. The current system is said to have developed because it represents the "most economical and efficient means of serving [the] market environment."[4] Critics pointing towards distribution inefficiencies from a cost standpoint are told to evaluate distribution as a system, based on its societal fit and the combination of both cost and performance.[5] Before embarking on a description of the current system, it therefore seems appropriate to trace briefly the historical development of the Japanese distribution system in order to attain a better understanding of today's realities.

During the feudal period of Japan, the country consisted of many small provinces that were largely self-contained. As a result, each province developed its own distribution system. Even after the abandonment of feudalism, the individuality and uniqueness of these provinces largely remained. Manufacturers who wished to penetrate these areas successfully had to develop appropriate distribution systems for each area. Since Japan consisted of about 500 regions, many manufacturers needed to develop wholesalers for each territory.

In addition to the feudal system, and perhaps of even more profound relevance, is the fact that the four main island divisions of Japan have restricted the mobility of both people and merchandise. As a result, suppliers needed to work with intermediaries in each of these areas since they were far better able to deal with customers in often remote places.

Over time, these constraints also resulted in a production system characterized by many small manufacturers who, in order to survive, needed the financing, distribution, and storage capabilities provided by wholesalers. These manufacturers were in need of middlemen to market their products widely. By using a wide, multilayered channel system, their products could be marketed at a fraction of the costs of direct sales. In addition, indirect sales by manufacturers avoided a logistical nightmare, since they would not require an astronomical number of contacts and deliveries. As the concept of channel geometry presented in Figure 12.1 shows, the use of intermediaries resulted in an additive, rather than a multiplicative, number of contacts and deliveries. Considering the number of manufacturers and retailers involved, this difference is of enormous cost significance. Rationally, the intermediary is contributing positively to the economic process, as long as the charges for its services are less than the savings incurred by the manufacturers due to the reduction of contacts.

Another reason for the current distribution system is the fact that Japanese manufacturers, in line with the general tendency toward specialization and division of labor, often preferred to specialize in their area of expertise, which is production, not distribution. Because of these factors, manufacturers and wholesalers frequently have made exclusive contracts.

Retailers in turn, being numerous, very small, and confined to very specific geographic regions, needed the inventory and distribution functions provided by wholesalers in order to survive. Again, this resulted in close relationships between retailers and wholesalers.

Other social developments contributed to the existence and expansion of small retailers who were dependent upon wholesalers. Japanese society has come to accept to some degree a "tolerated inefficiency" within its distribution system in

Figure 12.1
Channel Geometry Effects on the Distribution System

A. Direct Delivery by Manufacturers (3 Manufacturers, 10 Retailers)

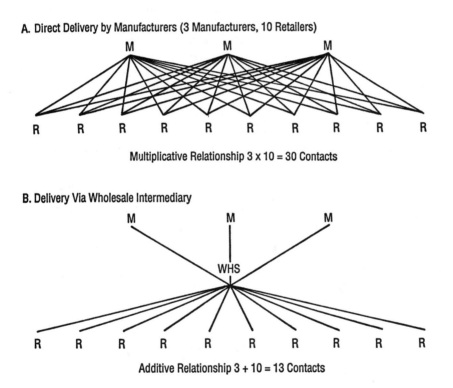

Multiplicative Relationship 3 x 10 = 30 Contacts

B. Delivery Via Wholesale Intermediary

Additive Relationship 3 + 10 = 13 Contacts

order to maintain employment and income flows. Retailing has come to serve to some extent as a "form of social welfare system."[6]

Since Japanese employees at retirement are paid a lump sum rather than an ongoing pension, this payment is often seen by the individual as an opportunity to set up a shop in order to be independent and to derive a steady income. As retirement often occurs at age 55, relatively early when compared to other industrialized countries, maintenance of income is important. Opening a retail store is the answer for many. The limited capital and experience of these retailers increase their dependence on wholesalers.

In addition to the interdependence among channel members as a Japanese way of life, which results in bonds forged by mutual obligation and service, there are other reasons for the current decentralized distribution system:

■ The financial needs of a system in which most business is done on the basis of promissory notes, debt financing, and consignments.

■ The need for risk reduction in distribution, which is achieved by the sharing of responsibility.

■ Specific system features such as rebates, discounts, and the unquestioned return of unsold goods.

■ The need to keep inventory constantly moving throughout the system.

■ The need to keep goods moving rapidly from producers to consumers.[7]

■ The expected long-term commitment by channel members in terms of time, money, and personnel, and the expected willingness to incur large investments devoted toward market entry with only a very limited return.

■ A system emphasis on secure and steady supply.[8]

■ Restrictions and limitations of retailers existing mainly in the areas of space and capital.

■ Existing geographic limitations, including narrow and congested streets that require small-lot deliveries in small vehicles.

■ The fulfillment of a social function for consumers by the distribution channel members.[9]

■ Strong demand by consumers for convenience and service.

■ Willingness on part of consumers to pay for service.[10]

Within all these constraints, a distribution system has developed that is fulfilling the demands placed on it. Functions are clearly distributed, as shown by the example of the cosmetics industry in Figure 12.2. Manufacturers concentrate

Figure 12.2
The Cosmetics Industry: An Example of Function Performance in the Channel System

Cosmetics Industry Channel Members

MANUFACTURER	INTERMEDIARY	RETAIL
Production	Order Taking	Selling
Advertising	Inventory Maintenance	Organizing Consumers
National Sales Promotion	Space Control at the Retail Level	In-store Promotion
Dealer Aids	Product Assortment	
Education of Dealers	Dispatching of Sales Support Personnel	
Financing	Area Marketing	
	Financing	

mainly on production and national promotional activities. Intermediaries interact closely with both the manufacturing and the retailing level; their work extends far beyond pure break bulk or product assortment activities. Retailers in turn concentrate on selling and promotional activities aimed at consumers within their area of business.

All the facets of the distribution system outlined so far will continually resurface in the remainder of this section. This short discussion was intended to delineate more clearly the historical growth of the Japanese distribution system and to demonstrate that, although due to its multilayered structure and its many uniquely Japanese procedural facets, foreign entry into this market may be perceived as tedious and difficult, this appears to be mainly the result of systemic constraints that, to a large extent, apply equally well to domestic products.

Notes

1. *Japanese Barriers to U.S. Trade and Recent Japanese Government Trade Initiatives* (Washington, D.C: Office of the United States Trade Representative, 1982), p. 71.

2. E. Ross Randolph, "Understanding the Japanese Distribution System: Explanatory Framework," *European Journal of Marketing,* Vol. 17, No. 1, 1983, p. 12.

3. *Japan's Distribution System and Options for Improving U.S. Access,* (Washington, D.C., U.S. International Trade Commission, June 1990), p. 2.

4. Yoshi Tsurumi, "Managing Consumer and Industrial Systems in Japan," *Sloan Management Review,* Fall 1982, p. 42.

5. Takafusa Shioya, "Japan's Distribution System is a Result of Economy, Society and Culture—MITI," *Business Japan,* August 1989, pp. 57–63.

6. "Strategies for Alleviating Recurrent Bilateral Trade Problems between Japan and the United States," in *The Japanese Non-Tariff Trade Barrier Issue: American Views and Implications for Japan-U.S. Trade Relations,* Report to the Japanese National Institute for Research Advancement, Arthur D. Little, Inc., May 1979, pp. 4–49.

7. Ibid., pp. 4–51.

8. Office of the United States Trade Representative, op. cit., p. 71.

9. Erich Batzer and Helmut Laumer, *Marketing Strategies and Distribution Channels for Foreign Companies in Japan,* (Boulder, Colorado: Westview Press, 1989), p. 49.

10. George Fields, "The Japanese Distribution System: Myths and Realitites," *Tokyo Business Today,* July 1989, pp. 57–59.

C H A P T E R

13

The Wholesale Sector

This chapter highlights the wholesaling activities taking place in Japan. Initially, the focus will rest with the wholesale structure, with a particular emphasis on channel members. Subsequently, the wholesaling process and the performance of the wholesaling function will be discussed.

The Wholesaling Structure

Wholesalers in Japan are oriented mainly, although not exclusively, along functional, geographic, and product dimensions. Functional wholesalers take on very specific roles as either export or import wholesalers or as primary, secondary, or even tertiary wholesalers. Geographic orientation expresses itself by a national or regional focus. Product orientation is often based on regional comparative advantage due to manufacturing concentration on particular product categories such as kimonos, pearls, or frames for glasses—much like, for example, the garment district in Manhattan or the diamond district in Amsterdam.[1]

Frequently, "wholesalers have a dominant position in the Japanese economy and have played a vital link in the selling chain for small manufacturers and retailers."[2] However, this holds true only for cases of low levels of concentration on the retail or manufacturing level. Conversely, in situations where concentration exists—as is the case, for example, in the electrical appliance industry, which has only a small number of major manufacturers—systematized forms of distribution are controlled by the manufacturers, often in the form of manufacturers sales centers, thus excluding or at least reducing the role of the wholesalers.

To manufacturers, "wholesalers have traditionally supplied managerial or marketing know-how as well as financial assistance to procure raw materials."[3] In addition, wholesalers are instrumental in performing break bulk functions in order to service the many small retailers who cannot order large quantities from manufacturers. This phenomenon of small orders is the result of insufficient storage space, since, due to high land prices, the cost of such storage space is often unaffordable for retailers. Wholesalers, particularly the older and more established firms, are at an advantage with regard to retailers and to new entrants into the wholesaling market, since they already have land and buildings that were acquired at lower prices and frequently have already been depreciated. Retailers' lack of storage space has resulted in a need for frequent replenishments. Since these replenishments are expected to be delivered rapidly, a need for close wholesaler proximity to retailers has arisen. This in turn has led to the development of large numbers of small wholesalers who are served by larger wholesalers.

Table 13.1 provides a breakdown of wholesalers by area of concentration in Japan in 1985, the latest year for which data are available. As can be seen, wholesale establishments are concentrated in the two prefectures of Tokyo and Osaka. These areas combined contain more than 27 percent of all Japanese wholesalers, with Tokyo having the clear lead with a 16.5 percent share of all wholesalers. Comparatively, all other regions drop off sharply in the extent of their wholesale activities.

A comparison between the Japanese and the U.S. wholesale structure (shown in Table 13.2) results in a number of interesting findings. Japan has more wholesalers than the United States, even though the United States has about 25 times the land mass of Japan and is twice as populous. The sector employs fewer people in Japan, but employment levels are rising. Aggregate annual sales of the wholesale sector, which were about 20 percent below the United States in 1982, appear to have risen rapidly by 1988 when measured in dollars. However, when adjusting for exchange-rate changes, an annual growth rate of less than two percent is found to exist.

Similarly, average annual sales per Japanese wholesaler seem to have vastly exceeded those of their U.S. counterparts, but in real terms have grown only slowly since 1982, when they were at a level of 78 percent of U.S. sales. The population per wholesaler in Japan is about half that in the United States, with a slightly decreasing tendency. Japanese wholesalers serve fewer retailers, with a declining tendency that is only partially attributable to a growth in the number of wholesalers. In addition, this fact does not reflect any difference in the size of the retailers served, a point that will be expanded on in the discussion of the retailing

Table 13.1
Wholesalers in Japan
(1985 data)

AREA OF CONCENTRATION	NUMBER OF ESTABLISHMENTS	PERCENTAGE
Tokyo	68,182	16.51%
Osaka	45,712	11.07
Aichi	28,313	6.85
Fukuoka	17,579	4.26
Hokkaido	16,599	4.02
Hyogo	14,896	3.61
Kanagawa	14,428	3.49
Shizuoka	13,286	3.22
Saitama	12,052	2.92
Hiroshima	10,847	2.62
Chiba	9,973	2.41
Kyoto	9,694	2.35
Others	151,455	36.67

SOURCE: Statistics Bureau, Management and Coordination Agency, *Japan Statistical Yearbook: 1989* (39th issue), 1989.

structure. Japanese wholesalers have, on average, only three-fourths of the number of employees of U.S. wholesalers. One must also remember that the Japanese computations include the very large trading houses, or *sogo shosha*, which, due to their large employment, may distort the picture somewhat.

Table 13.3 shows that more than 47 percent of Japanese wholesalers are small, with fewer than four employees. Large wholesalers, with 30 or more employees, make up only six percent of the total number of establishments. Even though some shifts between categories are visible from 1979 to 1988, they are minor and mainly point towards a slight reduction in medium-sized wholesalers. These figures clearly show that Japanese wholesalers tend to be fairly small, a fact that is corroborated by studies that indicate most wholesalers have fewer than nine employees.[4]

A comparison between combined wholesale and retail sales in Japan and the United States is presented in Table 13.4. It reveals that the ratio of wholesale to retail sales in Japan is more than double that of the United States, albeit with a declining tendency. The ratio of wholesalers to retailers could be adjusted for

Table 13.2
Comparing the Japanese and U.S. Wholesale Structure

	JAPAN		82-88	U.S.
	1982	1988	CHANGE	1982
Number of wholesalers	426,722	435,492	+2%	415,829
Number of employees	4,084,061	4,327,688	+6	5,282,000
Total annual sales ($ million)	1,600,547*	3,434,492*	+115	1,997,985
(yen, billion)	398.536	446.483	+12	
Annual sales per wholesaler, ($ million)	3.75*	7.89†	+210	4.8
(yen, billion)	.933	1.025	+10	
Population per wholesaler	287	281	-2	586
Number of employees per wholesaler	9.6	9.9	+3	12.7
Number of retailers per wholesaler	4.03	3.72	-8	4.6

*Calculated at the 1982 weighted average exchange rate of 249 yen = 1 U.S. $.
† Calculated at the 1988 weighted average exchange rate of 130 yen = 1 U.S. $.

SOURCES: Data for Japan: *Census of Commerce*, (Tokyo: Ministry of International Trade and Industry, 1989); Data for U.S.: *Statistical Abstract of the United States*, 1989 edition, (Washington, D.C.: U.S. Department of Commerce, 1989).

Table 13.3
The Size of Japanese Wholesalers in 1988

NUMBER OF EMPLOYEES	NUMBER OF ESTABLISHMENTS	PERCENTAGE 1988	(1979)
Small sized (1–4)	204,654	47	(46.5)
Medium sized (5–29)	206,211	47	(47.9)
Large sized (30 and over)	24,627	6	(5.6)
Total	435,492	100	(100.0)

SOURCE: *Census of Commerce* (Tokyo: Ministry of International Trade and Industry, 1989).

Table 13.4
Comparison of Wholesale Sales and Retail Sales in the United States and Japan

	JAPAN ¥ (billion)		U.S. $ (million)
	1982	1988	1982
Combined wholesale sales	398,536	446,484	1,997,985
Combined retail sales	93,972	114,840	1,065,917
Ratio wholesale : retail	4.24 : 1	3.89 : 1	1.87 : 1

SOURCES: Data for Japan: *Census of Commerce* (Tokyo: Ministry of International Trade and Industry, 1989; data for U.S.: *Statistical Abstract of the United States,* 1989 edition (Washington, D.C.: U.S. Department of Commerce, 1989).

more accuracy by deducting industrial transactions in which merchandise customarily flows directly from wholesalers to end-users. While doing so would reduce the ratio for Japan, a similar adjustment for the U.S. data would still result in the Japanese ratio of wholesalers to retailers being more than twice as high as the U.S. one. When compared to other industrialized nations, Japan clearly heads the list as the country with the highest wholesale to retail sales ratio.[5]

The Wholesaling Process

Japanese wholesale distribution is characterized by very close ties, both at a social and business level, between the participants in the distribution process: the manufacturers, the various levels of wholesalers, and the retailers. Socially, these close ties are a function of close personal relationships that are expressed through frequent visits and elaborate courtesies. The maintenance of these relationships is often far more important than the sales level of a particular product or short-term profitability. It includes the occasional provision of money to "send the son to school," frequent exchanges of gifts, friendly discussions, and very little direct pressure to sell. Violation of this relationship can have quite negative repercussions, as one U.S. supplier found out when his sales agreement with a large distributor was terminated. The Japanese distributor explained later that "when the U.S. sales manager visited some of my retail clients, not only did he keep on badgering them on how they had to increase sales, but he even refused to bow to them during the welcome greeting. He never understood the importance of our relationship, and that the retailers were really doing him a favor by carrying his product." Understanding these relationships and becoming part of them are, therefore, imperative for any firm wanting to do business successfully in Japan.

The existence of these strong bonds, however, should not be interpreted as doing away with competition. Wholesalers are expected by their retailers to be actively involved in business development, and pressures are exerted via them on the manufacturers to remain competitive in their product and price offerings.

The importance of the relationship among channel members is perhaps best highlighted with the example of a new product introduction. Often, such newly introduced products require the development of an entirely new distribution system. Even if this is not the case, the difficulty faced by firms new to the market is how to displace established products, particularly since space constraints are a major factor in the Japanese channel.

As a result, national introduction of a new product is quite expensive and time-consuming. The process frequently starts out with meetings across the country between the manufacturer (or importer) and some of the major wholesaling groups. These meetings—which often take the form of parties for presenting the product—are designed to capture channel input on marketing plans, and, most importantly, to establish or maintain channel relationships. The cost of these meetings can often mushroom into several hundred thousand dollars. While this expense may appear high, the manufacturer must incur it in order to obtain the cooperation of channel members.

For channel members to accept a new product, the manufacturer has to pursue both a push and a pull strategy. In instances of highly visible or desirable goods, channel members may be willing to share some of the introductory costs, but usually, the manufacturer must bear most of the burden. These initial expenses, however, do not guarantee success. Japanese wholesalers believe it important for manufacturers to follow up continuously on a first success of a product by improving it. If such improvements are not forthcoming, competitors are likely to enter the market with similar but lower-priced products, and the initial introductory success will be short-lived.

This is particularly the case for imports, since the emergence of a competitive Japanese product may result in current wholesalers of the imported product returning to their longstanding Japanese suppliers and dropping the imported product. The U.S. manufacturer of a shoe insole experienced such a development. After three years of quite costly market development efforts together with a Japanese wholesaler, the firm had reached a sales level of 3.8 million pairs. However, six months after product introduction, 12 comparable Japanese products had already been introduced. Since the U.S. firm was not able to improve its product substantially over time, its wholesaler made an exclusive agreement with a competing firm and terminated the relationship. Even though the U.S. firm found another distributor, its sales dropped significantly.

Importers into Japan need to recognize that in contrast to U.S.-style product development, which has placed major emphasis on the "giant leap forward" innovation, Japanese firms tend to have an incrementalist view of product development. This view emphasizes continual technological improvement aimed at making an already successful product better for customers. Incrementalism results in an increase in the speed of new product introductions, meets the competitive demands of a rapidly changing marketplace, and captures market share. It also affords an opportunity to gain experience, debug technological glitches, reduce costs, boost performance, and adapt designs to customer use. In other words, the marketplace becomes a virtual R&D laboratory for Japanese firms to gain production and marketing experience as well as to perfect technology.[6]

Once a product is successfully established, wholesalers and manufacturers are expected to supply a substantial amount of sales-support personnel for their products to retailers. This support staff often works in the retail store, wearing the store uniforms, but is paid by the wholesaler. In some department store areas, wholesaler-supplied personnel vastly outnumber store-employed personnel. In one case, 95 percent of the staff in the cosmetic section of a store consists of outside employees. One rationale behind this practice is that it is in the interest of the wholesaler (or manufacturer) to have personnel pushing its products, since its personnel are better able to explain the products to customers. In addition, the dispatching of personnel strengthens the mutual dependence and business relationship. Furthermore, the wholesaler and manufacturer can use the personnel to develop a direct mechanism for observation and feedback on consumer behavior. Such personnel assistance is, therefore, often an integral part of a firm's market research program.

Wholesalers are also expected to offer a very liberal return privilege to retailers, which extends not only to damaged merchandise but also to merchandise that does not sell easily. This privilege exists mainly to help small stores that cannot afford to keep unsold products in their limited space for long.[7]

One of the major reasons for the existence of wholesalers, of course, is the lack of storage and warehousing facilities in Japan. Even though the Japanese government has begun to introduce change by making warehousing facilities more widely available (a phenomenon that will be discussed in a later chapter), the cost of storage space is very high. In order to obtain space in an existing distribution center, tenants usually need to pay a number of charges on a square-meter basis. Examples of these charges are:

- Construction contribution fund: a one-time payment that is refundable only after 10 years with no interest payment.
- Security deposit: refundable only at the end of the lease with no interest paid.
- Monthly rent.
- Administrative charges.

Leases typically need to be signed for a minimum term of 10 years. Despite the substantial costs, vacancy rates at distribution centers are extremely low, with outside turnover often being less than two percent. The required long-term commitments to storage space are not seen as onerous by Japanese firms, since the entire distribution structure rests on the notion of long-term commitments of 10 years and more between channel members.

Because of the lack of storage space and its high cost, delivery lead time takes on major significance in the wholesaling process. Suppliers, particularly those from abroad, are chosen on the basis of responsiveness to orders by wholesalers. Even when sophisticated sales-forecasting systems are used, immediate manufacturer response to short-term orders is expected. As a result, factors such as short lead time and secure suppliers often can outweigh price competitiveness.

The financing activities of wholesalers also play a major role in the distribution process. Extended payment terms prevail in the wholesaling sector, with promissory notes frequently used for 90 to 120 days. In addition to straight financing,

wholesalers are also deeply involved in maintaining an elaborate system of rebates.[8] This system is highly individualized and, as a result, nontransparent. For
example, wholesalers, acting as agents for manufacturers, frequently receive commissions or rebates of two to five percent for invoicing and collecting from the
channel members. These commissions can be lower if the product is better
known. Larger wholesalers can also receive a rebate based on performance, very
similar to a cumulative discount, that often ranges between one and three percent.
For quick payment (within 30 days), three percent cash payment discounts are
frequently granted. Wholesalers are also rewarded by manufacturers for controlling disorderly markets by, for example, reducing aggressive discounting by retailers. Such rebates often are as high as two percent. Quantity discounts are also
granted for certain sizes of minimum orders and usually range between one and
two percent. While wholesalers can easily accumulate up to a 10 percent discount
this way from manufacturers, parts of these rebates need to be passed on to
retailers. Retailers, for example, may receive payments for being cooperative by
staying below an expected level of returned goods. Retailers may also receive
payments for quantity purchases and for participation in displays. Annual bonuses
paid by wholesalers to retailers can be two to three percent, and are often passed-
on payments that have previously been made for this specific purpose by the
manufacturer to the wholesaler.

As can be expected, various distribution routes may exist for similar goods.
The choice of a suitable channel of distribution results from considerations of
product characteristics, market characteristics, consumer purchasing behavior,
and size and competitive position of the firm. These considerations also affect
wholesale activities. For example, not all wholesalers engage in distribution activities; some mainly consolidate products and forward them to the large consumption centers to be distributed there. Other regionally specialized wholesalers offer
mainly a credit function without having a distribution network. Figure 13.1 provides an example of such different distribution alternatives, using the example of
soap.

Case 1 presents the most frequently used channel (60 percent of soap is distributed this way). Product deliveries are made from the manufacturer to a wholesaler, who in turn delivers to a retailer. Payment flows go from the retailer to the
wholesaler, who in turn pays the manufacturer.

Case 2 demonstrates another frequently used distribution process. Wholesaler
A sells the product to the smaller wholesaler B. Product flow, however, goes
directly from the manufacturer to wholesaler B. Wholesaler B in turn delivers to
the retailer. The fact that wholesaler B rather than A deals with the retailer is often
the result of an old and long-standing business relationship between B and the
retailer. Similarly, due to established relationships, B is more likely to deal with
A rather than going directly to the manufacturer. Payment flows go from the
retailer to wholesaler B, who in turn pays wholesaler A, who forwards payment to

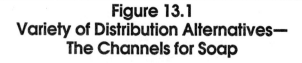

Figure 13.1
Variety of Distribution Alternatives—
The Channels for Soap

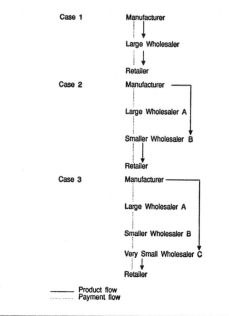

the manufacturer. Even though wholesaler A has not handled any of the physical product flow, it will receive a five percent commission on the sale from the manufacturer.

In Case 3, the channel is expanded by the addition of a very small wholesaler C. This wholesaler, even though virtually unknown to the manufacturer, receives its delivery of goods directly from the manufacturer. However, the manufacturer is willing to make this delivery only if wholesaler A guarantees the payment. Wholesaler A is able to do so because of its long established relationship with wholesaler B, who in turn maintains a trusted relationship with wholesaler C. The very small wholesaler in turn is able to deliver to retailers who often are quite far removed from any possible reach of the manufacturer (for example, a beach sales shop). Due to all these linkages, the manufacturer has ensured wide distribution of its product while minimizing the risk of nonpayment. The different wholesalers in turn have not incurred major expenditures since they have not participated in handling the physical product flow. In exchange for their credit facilitation, however, they are able to participate in the profits from the sale.

In summary, it can be said that wholesaling in Japan is characterized by the following salient dimensions:

- Major importance of traditional and social ties.
- Significant focus on service support throughout the channel.
- Use of the channel as a research tool.
- Important role of credit and financing.
- Sharing of risk and responsibility.
- Emphasis on rapid delivery and secure supplies.
- Great flexibility and accommodation of retailers.

Notes

1. William Lazer, Shoji Murata, and Hiroshi Kosaka,"Japanese Marketing: Towards a Better Understanding," *Journal of Marketing,* Vol. 49, No. 2, 1985, pp. 69–81.

2. *The Structure of the Japanese Retail and Distribution Industry 1981/82* (Tokyo: Dodwell Marketing Consultants, 1981), p. 71.

3. Ibid., p. 13.

4. Yoshi Tsurumi, "Managing Consumer and Industrial Systems in Japan," *Sloan Management Review,* Fall 1982, p. 41.

5. "Too Many Shopkeepers," *The Economist,* January 26, 1989, p. 70.

6. Michael R. Czinkota and Masaaki Kotabe, "Product Development the Japanese Way," *The Journal of Business Strategy,* November/December 1990, Vol. 11, No. 6, pp. 31–36.

7. Mitsuaki Shimaguchi and Larry J. Rosenberg, "Demystifying Japanese Distribution," *Columbia Journal of World Business,* Spring 1979, p. 36.

8. Mitsuaki Shimaguchi and William Lazer, "Japanese Distribution Channels: Invisible Barriers to Market Entry," *MSU Business Topics,* Winter 1979, Vol. 27, No. 1, pp. 57–58.

14

The Retail Sector

This chapter focuses on the retail structure in Japan. After discussing the types of intermediaries that carry out retail functions in the market and drawing comparisons with the United States, the retail process will be discussed.

The Retailing Structure

Japanese retailers are specialized along the dimensions of store type and products carried. The primary categories of retailers are department stores or *depato,* installment sales department stores, general merchandise stores, superstores (often also referred to as supermarkets or *supa*), convenience stores, and specialty stores. Within each of these functions, retailers can also be categorized by product specialty such as food, clothing, and household goods.

Department stores are among the most traditional retail institutions in Japan. Some date back several centuries, and many are linked with railroads and railway lines, as stores were typically established at important end terminals. No philosophical conflict arises between running a department store and running a railroad. As one store manager explained, "The railroad is there to serve the consumer as is the department store." This service orientation is typical of department stores. Both employees and customers are constantly reminded of it, and it is symbolized strongly each morning during the opening of the store. At the start of the business day, which is a ceremony that lasts several minutes, the chief officers of each store stand at the doors to welcome the customers with bows. All personnel—whether store employed or supplied by the other channel members—stand in the hallways bowing to the customers and thanking them for their patronage.

The department store assortment consists of merchandise priced in the medium to high range, with more and more luxury products being offered. Frequently, tenants within the buildings offer specialty goods. These tenants pay either rent and a commission on their sales or a commission only to the department stores.

Installment sales department stores are similar to their namesakes described above, except for the fact that most purchases there are handled on an installment plan, which many customers find attractive.

General merchandise stores and supermarkets are similar to each other in terms of merchandise, but they differ in size. Both handle a wide range of merchandise and initially competed on the basis of price. Increasingly, however, their main products have been traded up, and they frequently offer luxury items. Supermarkets offer general merchandise and carry a substantial variety of food products.

Specialty stores that concentrate on a deep product mix can be differentiated primarily by their product focus. One group offers luxurious items in great assortment, while another focuses on volume products and competes mainly on the basis of price.

Finally, convenience stores compose the vast majority of Japanese retailers. They are mainly small retail shops that cater to a very limited customer area. These small retailers are able to compete with larger stores due to their lower cost structure. Estimates are that in 1974 retailers with less than 10 employees operated with a cost factor of 21.6 percent of sales volume, while retailers with more than 100 employees needed a cost factor of 39.6 percent of sales. This ratio changes, however, if all calculatory costs (for example, salaries of the owners) are included for smaller retailers.[1]

Table 14.1 provides a breakdown of retailers by area of concentration using the latest available data from 1985. While there is a concentration of retailers in the areas of Tokyo and Osaka, it is substantially less than that of the wholesalers. As shown previously, Tokyo contains over 16.5 percent of all wholesalers, but only 9.2 percent of all retailers. Also, over 47 percent of all retailers are outside the major areas of concentration, whereas this was the case for only 36 percent of the wholesalers. This suggests that retailers are widely dispersed in Japan and often fulfill their function by being in quite remote areas.

A comparison between the United States and Japanese retail structure is shown in Table 14.2. Japan has only 16 percent fewer retailers than the United States. During the period from 1982 to 1988 the number of retail establishments has been gradually declining, reversing a steady buildup that had occurred during the 1970s

Table 14.1
Retail Locations in Japan

AREA OF CONCENTRATION	NUMBER OF ESTABLISHMENTS	PERCENTAGE
Tokyo	150,829	9.26%
Osaka	117,813	7.23
Aichi	82,372	5.06
Kanagawa	71,756	4.41
Hyogo	71,645	4.40
Fukuoka	65,262	4.01
Hokkaido	62,261	3.82
Saitama	59,856	3.67
Chiba	52,146	3.20
Shizuoka	50,669	3.11
Hiroshima	39,395	2.42
Kyoto	38,070	2.34
Others	766,570	47.07

SOURCE: Statistics Bureau, Management and Coordination Agency, *Japan Statistical Yearbook: 1989* (39th issue), 1989.

and early 1980s. The sector employs substantially fewer people than in the United States, but employment levels are on the increase. Aggregate retail sales grew very rapidly when measured in dollars, but were also strong when the exchange rate element was removed. The same held true for average annual sales per retailer, even when adjusting for the shrinkage in the retailer universe. In dollar terms, retail sales volumes in Japan are increasingly similar to their U.S. counterparts. The population served per Japanese retailer is still much smaller than in the U.S. but gradually increasing. Similarly, the average number of employees has been rising.

Table 14.3 supplies additional data on the size of Japanese retailers. Eighty percent of them have fewer than four employees, and only one percent fall into the larger size category. However, since 1979 there has been a clear drop-off in the number of smaller sized stores, most precipitously for stores that have only one or two employees,[2] resulting in a shift mainly into the medium sized category. Nevertheless, in relative terms, the number of large-sized stores has increased most during the same time, showing a growth of 20 percent. However, in comparison to the United States the largest Japanese department store chains are dwarfed

Table 14.2
Comparing the Japanese and U.S. Retail Structure

	JAPAN			U.S.
	1982	1988	82–88 CHANGE	1982
Number of wholesalers	1,721,465	1,619,752	-6%	1,923,200
Number of employees	6,369,426	6,851,335	+8	15,179,000
Total annual sales ($ million)	377,398*	883,380†	+134	1,065,917
(yen, billion)	93,972	114,840	+22	
Annual sales per retailer ($ million)	.219*	.545†	+149	.6
(yen, billion)	.055	.071	+29	
Population per retailer	71	76	+7	127
Number of employees per retailer	3.7	4.2	+14	7.9

*Calculated at the 1982 weighted average exchange rate of 249 yen = 1 U.S. $.
† Calculated at the 1988 weighted average exchange rate of 130 yen = 1 U.S. $.
SOURCES: Data for Japan: *Census of Commerce*, (Tokyo: Ministry of International Trade and Industry, 1989); Data for U.S.: *Statistical Abstract of the United States*, 1989 edition (Washington, D.C.: U.S. Department of Commerce, 1989).

Table 14.3
The Size of Japanese Retailers in 1988

NUMBER OF EMPLOYEES	NUMBER OF ESTABLISHMENTS	PERCENTAGE 1988	(1979)
Small sized (1–4)	1,296,444	80%	(85.1%)
Medium sized (5–29)	303,626	19	(14.1)
Large sized (30 and over)	19,682	1	(0.8)
Total	1,619,752	100	(100.0)

SOURCE: *Census of Commerce* (Tokyo: Ministry of International Trade and Industry, 1989).

by the sales volume of their U.S. counterparts. Only two Japanese retailers, Daiei and Ito-Yokado, would enter a listing of the 20 largest U.S. retailers.[3]

As far as imported consumer products are concerned, department stores and superstores are the primary carriers. Of total sales volume by these types of stores, imports typically account for 10 to 20 percent.[4] Since imports are frequently of high value, their share of total merchandise is substantially lower. Retailers other than department stores and superstores sell much less imported merchandise.

Large retailers typically have 50 percent retail margins, resulting in a mark-up of 100 percent. The average retailer receives 46 percent of its merchandise from primary wholesalers, 2 percent from secondary wholesalers, 35 percent from tertiary wholesalers, and 17 percent direct from manufacturers abroad.[5] While small retailers must obtain their goods from wholesalers, large retailers are sometimes able to buy directly from manufacturers.

In the case of imports, large retailers have two basic options: direct and indirect imports. The typical cost of direct importation is 35 to 45 percent of product price, which includes freight, insurance, customs clearance, inland transportation, and import duties. Using the 50 percent retail margin figure will, therefore, result in a store price of 250 to 290 percent of manufacturer's price. In the case of indirect imports through trading houses or agents, this percentage is generally higher, often reaching 350 percent of the foreign manufacturing price. Due to the resulting high prices, retailers are often faced with the need to either accept lower margins or abandon the importation of products. As a consequence, larger retailers tend more and more to purchase imports directly, and sometimes form their own importing group. One such group is the Allied Import Co., which was formed by Jusco, Uny, Izumiya, and Chujitsuya in 1979 for the purpose of joint importation of clothing, houseware goods, leisure goods, and foodstuffs.

Figures 14.1 and 14.2 provide examples of the benefits of direct versus indirect imports for a retail importing group. As can be seen, in both instances the flow of merchandise through various wholesaling levels has been reduced to comprise only a company internal wholesaler or distribution center. As a result, the importer has achieved savings of 25 percent and 17 percent, respectively. Using such shorter channels heightens the potential for imports. While the benefits of shorter channels apply equally well to domestic products, they are more difficult to implement since, other than for newly imported products where distribution channels are newly created for the retailer, domestic products are produced by established manufacturers who already have ties with channel members.

Figure 14.1
Example of Import Distribution Alternatives—
Distribution Route of Italian Spaghetti

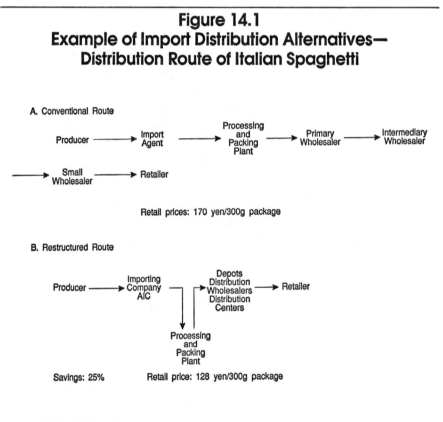

A. Conventional Route

Producer → Import Agent → Processing and Packing Plant → Primary Wholesaler → Intermediary Wholesaler → Small Wholesaler → Retailer

Retail prices: 170 yen/300g package

B. Restructured Route

Producer → Importing Company AIC → Depots Distribution Wholesalers Distribution Centers → Retailer

Processing and Packing Plant

Savings: 25%   Retail price: 128 yen/300g package

SOURCE: Allied Import Company.

Figure 14.2
Example of Import Distribution Alternatives—
Distribution Route of Bulgarian Strawberry Jam

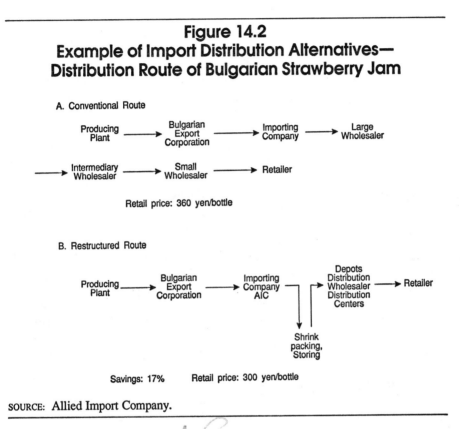

A. Conventional Route

Producing Plant → Bulgarian Export Corporation → Importing Company → Large Wholesaler

→ Intermediary Wholesaler → Small Wholesaler → Retailer

Retail price: 360 yen/bottle

B. Restructured Route

Producing Plant → Bulgarian Export Corporation → Importing Company AIC → Depots Distribution Wholesaler Distribution Centers → Retailer

↓ Shrink packing, Storing

Savings: 17%   Retail price: 300 yen/bottle

SOURCE: Allied Import Company.

The Retailing Process

Retailers in Japan are very demanding of manufacturers and wholesalers. As was mentioned previously, any returns of merchandise are expected to be fully accepted, even if there is no reason for the return other than the lack of sales capability. As a result, returns from retailers to wholesalers and subsequently to manufacturers are two to five times that in the United States. Retailers also expect substantial amounts of financing and frequent delivery of products from wholesalers and manufacturers. For example, food retailers expect delivery times for vegetables from cutting to store to be less than six hours.

However, retailers also offer substantial services to their clientele, and frequently take great pains to build a relationship with their customers. For example, one chain suggests to its customers that, once a week, all contents of the refrigerator should be replaced. Monday has been chosen by the store as the official replacement day on which discounts are offered. The store claims that if restocking is always done on Mondays, a family can save up to 30,000 yen per year. Some stores suggest eating habits for holiday periods or offer special weekend services. Others have a special awareness of family life. For example, since husbands are at home on weekends, heavy items that husbands usually carry and products that husbands like to eat are discounted on weekends.

One unique Japanese custom is that retailers frequently organize consumers into purchasing clubs. Consumers register with the retailer as members and their purchases are recorded. This mechanism of full cooperation between retailers and consumers permits the retailer to keep a record of the sales and to award a bonus to consumers who purchase given quantities during the year. At the same time, this type of record-keeping, if used systematically, provides invaluable insights into the shopping patterns of customers and permits the constant tracking of changing consumer tastes.[6]

Retailers, particularly the larger ones, take pride in offering integrated selling systems. For example, sports sections within department stores do not sell sports products in a pedestrian fashion. Constantly rolling video films, often supplied by the manufacturer, demonstrate equipment use on the shopping floor. Some stores even have a sports studio for their own video programming. Sports events are also transmitted and tapes of international tournaments are offered to customers. Stores often hire well-known former athletes as sales personnel who can provide customers not only with advice, but also with photographic opportunities and autographs.

Small retailers appeal to the convenience needs of consumers. Since until recently Japan's per capita income was too low to permit buying large quantities at one time, and since most Japanese households lack storage space and housewives prefer to shop several times a week in neighborhood stores, convenience often plays a major role. Besides the sociability of these shops, their owners perform special and personal services that supermarkets or department stores do not.[7] While the per capita income situation has changed, small retailers are still important. Since customers and retailers are frequently in locations that suffer from poor automobile access, most customers come by train, on foot, or on bicycle, and therefore can purchase and carry only limited quantities.

Given all the support retailers receive from other channel members and their close interaction with their customers, one would expect the retail business to be quite easy. However, this perception would be misleading. Retailing in Japan is an extremely competitive business, mainly due to the fact that the Japanese are among the world's most demanding customers. Their demands translate into exceedingly high requirements in terms of product freshness and in terms of a precise product–need fit. Perfect products are imperative. For example, pinstriped suits on which the stripes do not carry over perfectly from the shoulder to the front portion of the jacket are unacceptable to most consumers. Due to the competition consumers have very clear and defined ideas about the height, size, tastes, color and packaging of merchandise. All these requirements, of course, do not exclude the factor of price competition. However, in a trade-off situation, Japanese consumers are able to value the delivery of service and accept its higher cost.

As a result, many retailers are competing fiercely in the area of service. Department store personnel for example, will carefully check every part of a product a customer has selected before packaging it. If slight defects are found, the product will not be sold even if the customer is willing to take it, since long-range unhappiness could result. Great attention also is paid to packaging and wrapping, particularly during gift-giving seasons. As a result, the cost of packaging may sometimes exceed the value of the product sold.

Retailers, being very aware of the level of competition in their field, attempt to get ever closer to their customers. Retail stores frequently organize fairs that highlight specific products. Food retailers, which are still the mainstay of retailing because of Japanese dietary habits, try to communicate their customers' needs and demands by working closely with their farm products suppliers. Sometimes this cooperation goes as far as retailers suggesting different growing methods for farmers.

As a result of all the demands placed upon them, retailers expect at least the same, if not even more, service support for imported products than is obtained for domestic merchandise. However, if such support is given, products can be marketed effectively. The case of Rosenthal porcelain, imported from Germany, may serve as an example here. Rosenthal products, consisting mainly of porcelain, glass, and figurines, are very successful in Japan. Interestingly enough, these products are bought by customers more for gift-giving purposes than for personal use. The Rosenthal product mix in Japan is quite different from the mix in other countries. The main emphasis is on ornaments and tea items that can be given as gifts, and not on plates as in the United States. In order to be aware of what items are and could be in major demand and to adjust its production strategy accordingly, Rosenthal constantly conducts marketing research in Japan. Over the past 20 years the firm has developed a close relationship with Japanese retailers and frequently invites store personnel to visit the factories in Germany. In Japan itself, the company provides precise instruction for product display, even coordinating the colors within the displays. The firm has stationed employees permanently in Japan whose sole purpose is to work closely with retailers and distributors. Due to this very active representation, retailers can expect at least weekly contact with Rosenthal. In addition, the German company has developed a training program for Japanese retailers. Every year Japanese store employees go to the Rosenthal factory in Germany to learn about customer counseling. These trips, for which all expenses are paid by Rosenthal, last 10 days. Retailers are pleased with all that support and are eager to carry Rosenthal products, particularly since they offer comfortable profit margins.

While the support service activities offered by Rosenthal are unique even for Japan, they highlight the need for importers to display great sensitivity to Japanese service expectations.

Retailers, however, realize that such service emphasis results in substantial costs. They are fully willing to give new merchandise a chance by sticking with it for a prolonged period of time. Even if demand and profitability are low, many will devote portions of display space to products if they feel that the manufacturer and the channel members are willing to give the product long-range support and if they believe in the product's eventual success. It is not unheard of that retailers support products with no or minimal profit for several years in order to gradually introduce them to the public.

In summary, it can be said that retailing in Japan is characterized by the following dimensions:

■   Gradual decline of very small retailers.

■   Extremely high service orientation both on the intake and output sides.

■   Expectation and willingness for long-term commitment.

■   Close cooperation with channel members.

■   Substantial financing requirements.

■   Major "soft" research orientation.

Notes

1. Helmut Laumer, *Die Warendistribution in Japan* (Hamburg: Institut Fuer Asienkunde, 1979), p. 88.

2. Takafusa Shioya, "Japan's Distribution System is a Result of Economy, Society and Culture—MITI," *Business Japan,* August 1989, pp. 57–63.

3. Based on the 1989 *Fortune* listing of 50 largest U.S. retailing companies and *Diamond's Japan Business Directory,* 1989.

4. Retailing in the Japanese Consumer Market (Tokyo: JETRO Marketing Series 5, [undated]), pp. 42–3.

5. Laumer, op. cit.: 33.

6. Johny K. Johansson and Ijujiro Nonaka, "Market Research the Japanese Way," *Harvard Business Review,* May/June 1987, pp. 16–22.

7. Mitsuaki Shimaguchi and Larry I. Rosenberg, "Demystifying Japanese Distribution," *Columbia Journal of World Business,* Spring 1979, p. 35.

IV

Changes in the Distribution System

C H A P T E R

15

Changes in Wholesale Structure and Institutions

The preceding part provided an overview of the Japanese distribution system. However, even though the system is a result of tradition, it contains an inherent dynamism that results in numerous shifts and changes. This is not to say that the system has been or will be completely supplanted by something new, but rather that changes have come about that may have been little noticed but that indicate, and to some extent have already resulted in, major shifts in the functions, structure, and processes of the distribution system. These changes have come about not for the purpose of change per se, but as a reaction to the changing realities of the environment. Perhaps they are best characterized by Keiichi Konaga, the former director of the Industrial Policy Bureau of the Ministry of Trade and Industry:

> It remains to be seen whether the quantitative maturation of the Japanese economy, following two rounds of sharp oil price increases, shall lead to a better life for the consumer and produce a sense of fulfillment among the Japanese people. As consumer needs diversify with emphasis on quality rather than on quantity, it becomes increasingly important for the distribution industry to meet these needs.[1]

Structural Changes In Wholesaling

Many changes are occurring today in the Japanese wholesaling structure. Given the fact that distribution channels are the one market aspect that is slowest to change, trends need to be measured over the long term to be meaningful. Table 15.1 provides information about such trends, focusing on changes in the number of establishments and number of employees in six-year increments since 1970. Clearly the 1970s and the early 1980s were marked by very rapid growth in the wholesaling sector as far as establishments and employment is concerned. The fact that the number of establishments grew even more rapidly than did employment indicates that it was the small wholesaler where most of the growth occurred. However, since the mid-80s, this trend has been reversed on both scores. First of all, the growth rate of the number of establishments has been only minuscule, shrinking to less than 0.35 percent on an annualized basis. The growth in employment also declined substantially, but now almost triples the establishment growth rate. As a result, we find the size of wholesalers to be increasing for the first time in decades.

To some degree, this development may reflect natural market saturation. However, it also reflects that over the years, many larger retailers decided it would be more advantageous in the long run to go directly to the manufacturers instead. Also, by building their own distribution centers, these retailers were able to rely less on wholesalers.

As a result of these developments, the Japanese proverb "You can't fight the tonya" has lost much of its veracity today. The power of wholesalers as channel members is on the decline. Concurrent with this decline, the social status of

Table 15.1
Selected Trends in the Japanese Wholesale Industry

YEAR	NUMBER OF ESTABLISHMENTS	PERCENTAGE CHANGE	NUMBER OF EMPLOYEES (millions)	PERCENTAGE CHANGE
1970	255,974	—	2,861	—
1976	340,249	32.9%	3,513	22.8%
1982	426,722	25.4	4,084	16.2
1988	435,492	2.0	4,328	5.9

SOURCE: *Commercial Census* (Tokyo: Ministry of International Trade and Industry, 1981–1989).

wholesaling has decreased. This fact translates directly into personnel capabilities, since young people now prefer joining manufacturers or retailers rather than wholesaling firms.

Integration of Channels

The wholesaling sector, however, does not intend to give up its preeminent position without a fight. Increasingly, the sector is marked by both vertical and horizontal integration activities.[2] One trend that can be observed is the formation of manufacturer-wholesalers. These are firms that produce some merchandise, but subcontract the major part of their production. This is particularly the case in the men's and women's apparel industry, where manufacturers absorb the wholesalers. In some instances, however, wholesalers have absorbed smaller manufacturers and have begun to integrate forward into the retailing sector. Larger wholesalers also consolidate their activities with those of the secondary or tertiary partners in order to retain their market position. These integrated firms can pose problems for importers of merchandise, since, in good *keiretsu* fashion, a wholesaler is more likely to buy from its own manufacturing firm than from a foreign firm. Even if imported products are purchased, their distribution may be limited if the Japanese manufacturing arm of the wholesaler begins to produce a competing product. By the same token, wholesalers that grow larger and stronger through integration are more likely to establish their own international linkages and import more than smaller wholesalers.

However, this integration is not all-pervasive. There are still many manufacturers who produce small-lot merchandise for which wholesalers are necessary. Channel members at the manufacturing and the retailing level often still heavily depend on wholesaler financing. Also, many manufacturers, even if they could deliver certain goods directly, maintain their relationships with wholesalers for all transactions in order not to lose the small retailers they could not service if direct distribution were to be introduced and ties with wholesalers severed.

New Distribution Centers

Because of and in addition to these structural changes, the wholesaling process is also undergoing significant shifts. The migration to cities has resulted in greater urban congestion. Wholesalers and distributors located in the middle of urban centers face ever growing shortages of space and transportation problems. Also, a higher standard of living and a greater variety of goods place more demands on wholesalers. In addition, small wholesalers achieve less and less return on investment because they are often heavily involved in the financing of channel members and can sell only to small retailers.

Recognizing the problems of the wholesaling sector, the Japanese government began to legislate distribution improvements. One area in which these improvements gradually have come to bear is that of distribution zones, which result from the formation of government-sponsored joint ventures between small firms, large warehouse companies, and terminals for the purpose of creating more modern storage and warehouse facilities. The newly formed centers contain distribution warehouses, display space, office buildings, and space for parking. High warehouse buildings with direct truck access offer efficient space utilization. Warehousing space is fully climatized and largely automated. The administration of such centers also provides for maintenance, security, and common facilities such as cafeterias. As a result, tenants need to worry only about their own business. This specialization has a positive impact on firms. One company, for example, which previously needed to maintain 20 depots in Tokyo with a total of 400 employees, now reports occupying only one floor in a warehouse and working with 80 employees.

Apart from these government activities, manufacturers themselves are forming distribution centers and joining forces with other manufacturing firms to provide a wide assortment of products. Some manufacturers who in the past delivered exclusively to wholesalers are now, because of pressures from the retail sector, frequently delivering directly to retailers. While many wholesalers still receive a commission despite the direct flow of goods from manufacturers to retailers, these payments are often the result of old ties. As the older generation dies out, tradition is likely to become less pervasive and such payments may become less frequent.

New Transportation Structure

Another major change results from the fact that wholesalers in congested city areas are increasingly unable to provide competitive delivery service. A trend towards order-consolidation can be observed, particularly in the newer warehousing zones. New transportation companies are being formed exclusively for order-consolidation purposes. In cooperation with wholesalers or alone, such firms can achieve major transport economies. Transportation cost savings average about 30 percent and are sometimes as high as 60 percent. Consolidation is growing rapidly among wholesalers since nonusers are suffering severely from the competitive advantage of the low transportation cost of users. By turning over the delivery function to outside companies, the activities of many wholesalers change substantially. Rather than focusing mainly on delivery, they concentrate on providing financing, break bulk, and assortment services.

Many regional wholesalers are also changing their activities. As smaller manufacturers die out because they cannot compete against larger firms, the need for regional wholesalers diminishes, since the large firms often need no financing from small wholesalers. As a result, these wholesalers, rather than sending products from their region to large consumption centers as they have done in the past, begin now to bring in products from these centers for distribution in their region.

New Business Relations

Some of the traditions of the wholesaling process are also undergoing shifts. For example, the time-honored way of establishing ties and then sticking with one's business partners is changing. A reassessment of channels is increasingly done by channel participants, and switches are made if financially necessary.

Such a shift from traditional ways of doing business can perhaps be seen most clearly by looking at the emergence of cash-and-carry wholesalers, who are enjoying substantial rates of growth. Their primary competitive tool is price. These firms aim at those retailers that do not require financing or delivery service. Frequently, their main customers are the very small retailers who come every day to purchase products in small quantities. These wholesalers refuse to accept returns from retailers and suggest instead that they discount slow-selling merchandise. No personal linkages are developed and no rebates or bonuses are granted.

In their dealings with manufacturers, these cash-and-carry wholesalers are similarly unconventional. No personal relationship is developed here either. These firms deal with many small manufacturers and select suppliers only on the basis of product and price competitiveness. While this method of doing business results in low prices, such cash-and-carry wholesalers often cannot sell national brand merchandise, since many large and well-known manufacturers are unwilling to sell to them. However, in spite of this handicap, these firms have annual inventory turnovers as high as 30, while conventional consumer goods wholesalers achieve an average annual inventory turnover of seven. Increasingly, these pioneers are also handling their own importing and exporting, and therefore can be valuable allies of a foreign manufacturer.

In sum, the major changes in wholesaling are occurring along the following dimensions:

■ An increased focus on competitiveness results in a major emphasis on efficiency.

■ In order to retain market power, substantial horizontal and vertical integration is taking place.

■ These changes in structure and process tend to deemphasize business customs that are the result of traditions.

■ While many channel members, in spite of changes in activity, still aim to maintain old behaviors, these changes have made room for reorientation of current wholesalers and the emergence of new types of channel partici-pants.

■ All present factors indicate a period of transition where time is on the side of the new and efficient.

Notes

1. Keiichi Konaga, "Future of Japan's Distribution Industry," *Dentsu Japan Marketing Advertising,* Spring 1984, p. 1.

2. William Lazer, Musata Shoji, and Kosaka Hiroshi, "Japanese Marketing: To-wards a Better Understnading," *Journal of Marketing,* Vol. 49, No. 2, Spring 1985, p. 79.

16

Changes in Retail Structure and Institutions

Significant changes are occurring in the retail sector as well. Table 16.1 shows selected trends in the Japanese retailing system over a 20-year period. The number of establishments, which was growing rapidly in the 1970s and continued to grow in the early 1980s, has declined in the second half of the 1980s. Concurrently, the number of employees has also slowed in its high growth rate, but continues to grow in spite of the decline in the number of establishments. As a result, one can conclude that the size of the stores must be growing, a conclusion that is born out by a look at the sales floor area per store, shown in Table 16.2, which has consistently risen over time. However, the rate of increase in the sales floor area has slowed in the 1980s, which indicates that the strong push in the growth of larger stores has diminished in recent years.

The Big Store Law

This development, of course, is no accident. While some trace the lack of store growth back to changes in consumer behavior and demand, others claim that the primary reason for this development lies with the Large-Scale Retail Store Law.

Table 16.1
Selected Trends in the Japanese Retail Industry

YEAR	NUMBER OF ESTABLISHMENTS (millions)	PERCENTAGE CHANGE	NUMBER OF EMPLOYEES (millions)	PERCENTAGE CHANGE
1970	1,432	—	4,650	—
1976	1,614	12.7%	5,580	20%
1982	1,721	6.6	6,370	14.1
1988	1,619	-6.0	6,850	7.5

SOURCES: Authors' calculations based on *Commercial Census* (Tokyo: Ministry of International Trade and Industry, 1989) and Japan Economic Institute, *JEI Report 14B,* (Tokyo, April 1989, p. 12).

Table 16.2
Sales Floor Area/Store

YEAR	SALES FLOOR AREA/STORE (m^2)*	PERCENTAGE CHANGE
1968	34.2	—
1976	48.8	43%
1982	55.4	13.5
1988	63	13.7

*1m^2 = approximately 10ft^2

This legislation has its roots in the 1956 Department Store Law, which was passed to protect small- and medium-sized retailers from department stores. The original law, which regulated the opening of department stores and increases in their size, applied to stores that had a selling area of over 1,500 square meters. It provided for a council of consumers, academics, representatives of small- and medium-sized stores, and representatives from local department stores under the aegis of the local chamber of commerce to evaluate all plans for new stores. Acting on various justified and unjustified fears expressed by their members, many of these councils turned out to be an onerous burden for companies planning to open department stores.

In order to circumvent the law, stores were opened with slightly less than 1,500 square meters of selling space, and some chains formed groups of companies that would purchase a building and open "different" stores on each floor, with each floor being slightly less than 1,500 meters. Since the law applied to stores occupying buildings with a total space of over 10,000 square meters or a total selling space over 6,000 square meters, usually four "different" stores were found in any one building.

Because of this circumvention of the Department Store Law, in March 1974 the Large-Scale Retail Store Law was passed, with the expressed intent of promoting the development of a "balanced" retail industry. The law attempted to reconcile the interests of large retail stores with the interest of smaller retailers in the same locality, while at the same time giving due consideration to the interests of consumers. Companies planning to open stores with a sales floor space of over 1,500 meters were now required to notify the Ministry of International Trade and Industry of their plans. In addition, no more subdivision of buildings was possible. Local area councils known as Commercial Activities Adjustments Boards were now in charge of deciding the restrictions to be placed on any new large stores with regard to sales floor space, closing hours, the proposed opening date, and the number of store holidays per month.

In 1979, the Large-Scale Retail Store Law was amended to apply to stores with sales floor space exceeding 500 square meters. While the procedures of this amendment were generally the same as those of the previous law, the newly covered smaller stores were required to notify the local prefectural government rather than MITI. This change in turn resulted in some local prefectures and city councils passing additional ordinances that restricted the establishment of stores with a size of 300 or even 200 square meters.

All these regulations required registration and notification, but not approval by MITI. On the surface, therefore, they appeared to have only a minor impact on the further development of larger stores. This, however, was not the case. MITI would only accept a notification if the applicant was able to show unanimous consent from the local boards. Since these boards or councils are composed of a wide variety of individuals in order to be better sounding boards for MITI, it was difficult for any applicant to obtain such consent. As a result, applications became excessively time-consuming and costly. The process, which on paper was to take only two years, seemed to be never-ending. For example, Izumiya waited 10 years to open a store in Kyoto, while Ito Yokado went through a nine-year routine just to locate one store in Shizuoka City.[1] Unknown is the number of firms that despaired in light of the lengthy process and either withdrew their application or never filed one in the first place.

Even when the application process was completed successfully, onerous operating requirements could make a viable project economically unfeasible. The regulatory process could, for example, stipulate the operating hours, number of days a store needed to be closed, maximum floor space, or other restrictions that would provide smaller retailers with a better competitive chance. Given sufficiently burdensome requirements, any store opening could be made financially unattractive.

The overall result of all these measures was that the opening of new large stores plunged. Foreign firms and governments grew very concerned about this development. For one, these onerous regulations inhibited the opening of large retail stores in Japan to such a degree, that no foreign-owned or -managed retail store has ever opened in Japan under the Large-Scale Retail Store Law.[2] As a result, one avenue for forward integration by any single foreign retailer, manufacturer, or group of producers from abroad was closed.

Of equal importance was the fact that the inhibition of large-store growth also affected the market penetration of foreign products. Large stores tend to import more of their merchandise from abroad, purchase in order quantities that are more likely to make imports economically feasible, and develop expertise in the direct importation of foreign products. Over time, large stores had become the primary channel to expose Japanese consumers to imports. The volume of foreign sales grew to over 16 percent of total sales in larger stores, with continuing increases projected. By contrast, the share of imports in small shops was infinitesimally small and often totally nonexistent.[3]

Because the international repercussions of the Large Store Law, in the 1980s the international trade community, mainly outside of but also within Japan, began to mount a vigorous campaign against it. MITI attempted to assuage concerns by either denying the inhibitory effect of the measure or by promising change. Yet it took numerous recommendations by commissions, panels, research teams and individuals to initiate the consideration of change.

In 1990, responding in large measure to discussions held with U.S. trade negotiators in the Strategic Impediments Initiative (SII), MITI announced several specific measures that would alter the Large Store Law and its administration. The length of the application process was to be reduced to a maximum of 18 months from start to finish, store expansions of less than 100 square meters that mainly served the promotion of imports were to be exempted from the application process altogether, and local government bodies were to adjust their policies with regard to large stores to conform with the guidelines issued by MITI.

While certainly necessary, these changes are not yet a reality. Clearly, the Large Store Law has played a major role in protecting the small-scale retail sector in Japan. Reorganization of such a sector is likely to precipitate social and political tension. Continued obstacles can, of course, be expected from the small shopkeepers. As stated earlier, small-scale retailing is, to a large degree, an activity to be engaged in after retirement. A glance at the Japanese population age pyramid indicates that in the coming decades, the number of retirees is likely to increase sharply. As a result, the pressure to increase the number of smaller shops appears to rise, together with the political influence of such retailers.

Not unexpectedly, Japan's political institutions are not necessarily in agreement with MITI's plans. Japanese unions have vowed opposition, as has the Ministry of Home Affairs.[4] Even within MITI itself conflict is visible when one scrutinizes the "vision" for Industrial Policy in the 1990s. Here, the ministry calls for "restrictions on further congestion in Tokyo by examining such measures as limiting government support for large-scale projects to retard the demand for new land," and "transferring authority from the national government to local governments."[5]

It appears at this time that the desire and pressure for change in the law has gathered sufficient momentum to gradually bring about some shifts. While swift, major alterations are unlikely to occur, the focus of attention seems sharp enough to prevent another market opening dimension from sinking into oblivion. The proposals for store openings by Sears and Toys R Us will serve as a watershed for things to come.

The resulting benefits might not be as focused as was the source of pressure for change. While an increase in larger stores is likely to augment the volume of U.S. exports to Japan, clearly exports from other countries, particularly in Europe and the newly industrializing nations, will be prime beneficiaries as well. The bottom line, however, chiefly will be an increase in competition and choice for the Japanese consumer.

The Emergence of New Retail Structures

Over time, shifts in the market shares of different types of retail establishments are becoming visible. Table 16.3 provides an overview of these shifts.

Traditional retailers, such as department stores, general merchandising stores, shopping centers and food supermarkets appear to struggle to hold their own. These intermediaries focus on staying with their mission and conducting business more efficiently. For example, in order to import more efficiently, many of these retailers have increased their involvement in direct imports. By eliminating the usual channels controlled by domestic trading firms and import businesses, these retailers cut their purchasing cost and save the margins usually taken by such middlemen. As a result, by 1988, direct imports accounted for around 40 percent of the total spent on imports.[6]

By contrast, other intermediaries are developing new retail structures. These are chain stores, discount stores, and nonstore retailers, which either restructure their current internal operations to gain competitive parity with their larger brethren, or introduce new forms of retailing altogether. These retailers show major annual growth rates and market share gains. Discount stores achieve most of their success based on price, a feature that will be discussed in Chapter 24.

Table 16.3
Changes in the Sales by Different Types of Retail Business
(million yen)

TYPE OF RETAIL BUSINESS	1984 (SHARE, %)	1985 (SHARE, %)	AVERAGE ANNUAL GROWTH RATE (%)	1988 (SHARE, %)	AVERAGE ANNUAL GROWTH RATE (%)
Department stores	7,153,669 (7.3)	7,982,465 (7.8)	3.7	9,551,819 (8.3)	6.2
General merchandising stores (GMS)	9,222,128 (9.8)	11,129,548 (10.9)	6.5	*12,133,000 (in 1987)	4.4
Shopping centers	9,071,800 (9.7)	10,620,700 (10.4)	5.4	*11,895,400 (in 1987)	5.8
Voluntary chains (VC)	*7,908,000 (8.4) (in 1981)	10,356,600 (10.2)	7.0	12,850,000 (11.2)	7.5
Franchise chains (FC)	3,907,191 (4.2)	4,515,362 (4.4)	4.9	*5,939,078 (in 1987)	14.7
Convenience stores	2,177,609 (2.3)	3,382,902 (3.3)	15.8	N.A.	N.A.
Food supermarkets	4,120,066 (4.4)	4,788,381 (4.7)	5.1	N.A.	N.A.
Volume-sales electric appliance outlets	745,100 (0.8)	1,059,800	12.5	1,609,300 (1.4)	14.9
Door-to-door sales	1,580,000 (1.7)	2,150,000 (2.1)	10.8	*2,270,000 (in 1986)	5.6
Mail-order business	640,000 (0.7)	830,000 (0.8)	9.1	1,150,000 (in 1987)	17.7
Total sales	93,971,191	101,719,064	2.7	114,828,936	4.1

SOURCES: Statistics on the Sales of Large-Scale Retail Stores; Japan Chain Store Association; Japan Shopping Center Association; Japan Voluntary Chain Association; Japan Franchise Chain Association; Census of Commerce; Nippon Electric Big-Store Association; Japan Direct Marketing Association; Japan Direct Selling Association.

NOTE: Some retail services appear in more than one category.

Chain stores and nonstore retailers, however, present fundamental structural shifts that deserve more exploration here.

The Development of Chain Stores

As was highlighted earlier, the small retail store sector of the Japanese economy is under pressure, both internal and external. Yet, due to the societal structure of Japan, together with the economic and political importance of small-scale retailers, these types of intermediaries are not about to disappear. Rather, they are likely to continue to survive and even prosper, albeit under different organizational and structural circumstances. MITI's industrial policy bureau sees the future for smaller retailers mainly in the organization of small stores into voluntary and franchised store chains, where small shopkeepers can benefit from technological innovations such as computerized inventory control and merchandise selection while being able to retain their individualized operations and some measure of independence.

Sure enough, this governmental vision is implemented by the private sector. Currently, more than 50 chains have over 18,000 outlets. Chain store sales volume surpassed 18.7 trillion yen in 1988 and continues to grow rapidly. Particularly in light of projections that large retailers are planning to increase their 1991 investment by 81 percent over the 1986–88 level, and that new floor space in 1991 is expected to be up 93 percent over the average new footage in 1986–1988, smaller retailers are scrambling to sign up for franchise agreements. One main advantage of these smaller retailers is the fact that they already have ongoing operations and available store space, and are thus less affected by the astronomical land prices that have to be faced by the expanding large retailers.

Chain stores are typically located in residential areas, carry only a limited range of goods needed daily, and are open long hours. These stores cater primarily to working singles and couples. In most instances the stores are owned by an individual on a franchise or volunteer basis. Chain management provides owners with help and training in the areas of management techniques, stocking policies, and service structure.

For example, Ito-Yokado, which licensed the 7-Eleven name in 1974 (and is now a major owner of the U.S. chain), provides computerized stock control and a range of new services that allow customers to send faxes, arrange overnight deliveries, and pay their gas bills. Even though retailers signing on to an Ito-Yokado franchise have to commit themselves to pay the firm 45% of sales in royalties for 15 years, 7-Eleven's more than 3,600 outlets average twice the turnover of their competitors.[7] In 1989, net sales of the 7-Eleven chain amounted to $5.4 billion. Key to such success is the constant fine-tuning of merchandise on display with consumer demand. For example, within one half year, 1,800 items out of 3,000 to 3,500 are replaced in response to changing customer needs.[8]

Between 350 to 400 new outlets are expected to open every year, and analysts claim that the density of such chain stores could more than double from the present one per 1,350 households before profits start to suffer.[9]

Other chain stores are My Shop, Lawson, Sunshop Yamazaki, Sun Chain and Family Mart. A large voluntary chain is Kei Mart, whose management also works with sophisticated technology to meet consumer needs. This chain introduced the voluntary chain information system (VOIS), which provides selling information from all its stores and permits the purchasing of 68 percent of its merchandise by headquarters.

Such centralized purchasing is a key feature of most chain stores. Despite the small size of any individual member store, the combined purchases often make a chain the largest buyer of any particular brand. The resultant economies of scale bring a major price benefit to the chain members. For imports into Japan, however, this centralized purchasing has yet to translate into major direct sales. For example, 7-Eleven reports that it directly imports only three items from the United States for its stores in Japan: whiskey, raw ingredients for potato chips (potatoes from Idaho) and Budweiser beer. The firm claims its purchasing patterns, particularly the low level of imports, are dictated by consumer preferences, especially for freshly-made prepared foods.[10]

It stands to reason, however, that over time further search for efficiency and a broadening of the product base into nonfast-food merchandise will presage larger increases in the potential for import penetration of such chain stores than of the independent small-scale retail store. Particularly, the use of detailed inventory tracking systems will precipitate that products are not kept on the shelf because of long-standing business relationships, but rather based on performance and turnover.

The Emergence of Nonstore Retailing

Two major trends in the nonstore retailing area stand out. These are direct marketing and mail order retailing. The direct marketing picture is somewhat bimodal. Door-to-door sales, which were growing rapidly in the early 1980s, have slowed to an annual growth rate of less than two percent.[11] In part due to the Japanese culture, which is less open to home visits by strangers, as well as to changing societal patterns, such as the increasing employment of women, this retail avenue seems to decrease in its popularity. By the same token, companies using the home party approach, which gathers friends, have been expanding rapidly. Some foreign beneficiaries have been Amway, Shaklee, and Tupperware. Amway, for example, achieved annual growth rates of 50 percent in three consecutive years, resulting in 1988 sales of more than $500 million and the rating as the seventh-fastest-growing company in Japan.[12]

Another firm experiencing major success in its direct marketing approach is Franklin Mint of the United States. The company uses primarily print advertisements to expand its customer base and direct mail to communicate with its customers. By 1986, the Japanese market had become the company's biggest revenue source outside of the U.S. Even though many of the firm's U.S. offerings are also sold in Japan, today almost 65 percent of its sales result from products developed especially for the Japanese market.[13] In spite of these success stories, and the rapid growth of some direct marketing activities, however, foreign companies account for less than one percent of Japan's direct marketing volume.[14]

Mail order retailing has also grown very rapidly, reporting annual growth rates of over 17 percent. In a 1985 survey of married women by MITI, nearly 72 percent of the respondents claimed that they used catalogs, with more than half having done so in the previous 12 months. On average, each woman had shopped by mail three times.[15] The 1989 introduction of lower catalog mail rates by the postal service should provide an additional boost to that industry.

In spite of all this growth, however, mail order market acceptance is still in its introductory stage in Japan. It is estimated that between 2,000 and 3,000 firms are involved in the mail order business. However, mail order sales represent only one percent of total retail sales in Japan, compared to about five percent in West Germany and 14 percent in the United States.[16] Of this market, foreign firms hold a market share of less than one percent.[17]

Typical products marketed by mail are furniture, clothing, accessories and jewelry, sporting goods, and shoes, with most prices in the 10,000 to 40,000 yen range.[18] In order to attract more customers, the industry is presently undergoing a major service delivery transformation for foreign products. At a very basic level, mail order goods are available through several retail chains that have opened foreign mail order departments. For example, Yunyua, a mail order unit of the Seibu group, stocks catalogs from about a thousand different sources such as Sheplers, Tiffany, Boston's Museum of Fine Arts, Bloomingdale's, Sears, the British Museum, and L.L. Bean. About 70 are for sale. The customer simply browses through the catalog and makes a selection.[19] The selection is checked as to its availability via air mail. Once availability is established, the customer pays for the selection in yen, returning several weeks later when the merchandise has arrived.

In a similar fashion, mail order catalogs are sold through bookstores. The Tokyo-based Adanac Trading Company, for example, published in 1988 an edition of "Canadian Dream Mail-Order Magazine," featuring a wide variety of Canadian consumer products. The 100,000-copy first edition was retailed through bookstores at 1,800 yen. Credit-card orders from this edition topped 100 million yen by 1989.[20]

More sophisticated are the efforts of Matsuzakaya, a Nagoya department store that has had a long-standing mail order relationship with Quelle, Germany. In order to reduce the lag time between customer selection and receipt of merchandise, Matsuzakaya has established a direct satellite link with Quelle. Customer catalog selections are now transmitted directly to Quelle via computer terminals located in the stores. After a check for availability via the on-line system, merchandise can be sent off immediately, thus reducing total order lag-time to less than two weeks.[21]

Even more technologically advanced are the television shopping opportunities. One development is a two-way interactive cable television system by HI-OVIS, supported by MITI. This project, which was initiated in 1976, permits the two-way transmission of both voice and picture. It allows individuals to request the showing of specific videotapes on their television sets. In addition to offering individualized programming, HI-OVIS also provides retail functions. Companies are provided with time slots to explain products and interact with viewers. A teleshopping program is offered in which viewers can examine merchandise and compare prices.

Already commercially viable is a program on the Fuji Television Network that introduces new foreign products directly to the Japanese audience. Viewers of the show, aired for 90 minutes at midnight every third Friday, can phone a toll-free number to order directly from the network's Fujisankei Living Service, which looks after importation, payment, and delivery. So far, viewers have been offered everything from a castle in France at 300 million yen to designer bags for kids at 5,000 yen.[22]

Of visionary quality is the concept of the World Shopping System, developed by the Distribution System Development Center. Shown in Figure 16.1, this system is based on an on-line communications network with links between Japan and other nations. Built around a computer-driven database of foreign products and suppliers, it can provide access to participating department stores and supermarkets. In order to make payment both more convenient and efficient, the network will also include links to major credit card firms and financial institutions. In support of this project, MITI requested a 20 million yen appropriation for further study.[23]

In spite of these structural and technological developments in the mail order field, companies still encounter substantial difficulties in using this marketing tool. Mailing costs are still very high. Mailing lists are often hard to obtain since they are not rented or sold as often as in the United States.[24] In addition, the majority of mailing lists in Japan are not computerized, and for those that are, there is no standard electronic format. What's more, even lists in the same format are difficult to work with because as many as four different alphabets (two phonetic Japanese systems, the Roman alphabet, and Chinese characters) are used, and data fields written in different systems are not always compatible.[25] Nevertheless, changing lifestyles, growing acceptance of the mail-order concept, improved delivery, service and return systems and more sophisticated technology

Figure 16.1
The World Shopping System Network

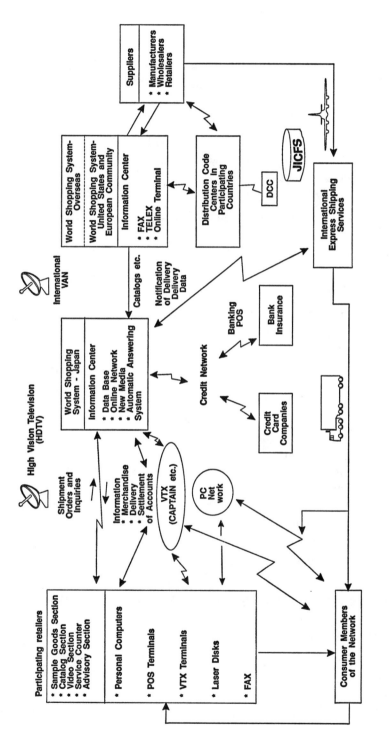

SOURCE: *Interim Report on the World Shopping System Concept*, the Distribution System Development Center, May 1989.

will make this form of nonstore retailing a prime one to consider for the foreign marketer.

Notes

1. Sixth Workshop on Japan's Distribution Systems and Business Practices, MIPRO, October 27, 1989, p. 25.

2. *Japan's Distribution and Options for Improving U.S. Access,* Report by the U.S. International Trade Commission, June 1990, p. 68.

3. USITC Report, op. cit., p. 73.

4. USITC Report, op. cit., p. 77.

5. *International Trade and Industrial Policy in the 1990s,* Ministry of International Trade and Industry, Tokyo, July 5, 1990, pp. 30-31.

6. *Sixth Workshop on Japan's Distribution Systems and Business Practices,* MIPRO, October 27, 1989, p. 8.

7. "Japanese Retailing: Jumping the Gun," *The Economist,* April 21, 1990, p. 76.

8. Sekikawa Hitomi, "7-Eleven Japan Develops About 2000 Stores," Distribution Code Center, The Distribution Systems Research Institute, Tokyo, February 9, 1984, p. 1.

9. *The Economist,* op. cit.

10. *U.S. ITC Report,* op. cit., p. 80.

11. *Retail Distribution in Japan,* Tokyo: Dodwell Marketing Consultants, 1988, p. 48.

12. Ronald E. Yates, "Patience Pays Off for U.S. Firm's Business in Japan," *The Washington Post,* January 28, 1990, p. C1.

13. A. Robert Deter, "Mail Order Marketing Starts Delivering Results," *Tradepia International,* No. 41, 1990, p. 16.

14. *U.S. ITC Report,* p. 43.

15. "Japan's Distribution System: The Next Major Trade Confrontation?" *Japan Economic Institute,* March 17, 1989, p. 8.

16. *Retail Distribution in Japan,* op. cit., p. 45.

17. *U.S. ITC Report,* p. 43.

18. *Retail Distribution in Japan,* op. cit., pp. 46–47.

19. Robert E. Weigand, "The Gray Market Comes to Japan," *Columbia Journal of World Business,* Fall 1989, p. 20.

20. "New 'Storeless' Market Gateways," op. cit., p. 3.
21. Kiodo News Release, Tokyo, March 1984.
22. "Mail Order Sales," *Focus Japan,* August 1989, p. 4.
23. Sixth Workshop on Japan's Distribution System and Business Practices, op. cit., pp. 27–29.
24. "Can this Catalog Company Crack the Japanese Marketing Maze?" *Business Week,* March 19, 1990.
25. A. Robert Deter, op. cit., p. 17.

C H A P T E R

17

Changes in Consumer Behavior

In spite of the claims by some researchers that "the facts appear to be that little distributive change has occurred [in Japan] and that improvement in this sector will take a great deal of time,"[1] we see shifts of substantial proportions in the retailing process. Many of them are primarily the result of changing consumer behavior. Due to changes in income levels and the desire for more originality, Japanese consumer needs have diversified over the years. Many consumers have already satisfied most of their demand for physical goods and have filled the available space in their homes. Increasingly, consumer demand is focusing on nonproduct areas, as can be seen in the gradual trend in consumer spending patterns. An increasing proportion of expenditures goes toward services, while the product portion of consumer expenditures is decreasing. As a result, the mission of larger retailers is changing. Rather than being simple sellers of products, they have become marketers of culture. Increasingly, consumers prefer to rely on brand names rather than on retail personnel advice.[2] Consumers have become more accepting of the self-service concept, but, at the same time display a clear trend toward the demand for convenience. Other trends are:

- A shorter work week, which permits more time for leisure activities such as sports and pleasure trips.

- A renewed orientation toward crafts.

- A sharp increase in consumer acceptance of financing.

- A renewed focus on cultural events—people again taking courses in literature, flower arranging, and calligraphy but doing so side-by-side with computer courses.[3]

- A fashion orientation within households that focuses not just on clothes, but also on furniture and eating utensils.

- An increase in disposable income and a willingness to spend, particularly since empty-nest housewives enter the labor market in order for the household to be able to afford luxury services.

- An increased focus on spiritual enrichment rather than on products alone.

Concurrent with those developments in consumer behavior, retailers are also seeing changes in employee attitudes. While the willingness to serve is still extremely high, some gradations have become visible. For example, in the department store opening ceremonies, younger employees can be observed to bow not quite as long and not quite as deeply as the older ones. Employees are increasingly interested in job diversity and in leisure time and hobby activities. This fact is reflected in the flexible job program initiated by Seibu. The Seibu Group, which comprises 100 companies and employs nearly 77,000 people, offers its workers the opportunity to divide their five-day work week between two jobs, to work on the side on their days off, or to change jobs without losing their seniority—as long as these shifts are made within the group.

More and more retailers, particularly the larger ones, are restructuring their offerings and providing more services. Frequently, one can hear Japanese executives refer to their stores as culture centers. Services such as travel bureaus, beauty shops, health programs, real estate, insurance, tax advice, legal services, and evening courses are becoming increasingly part of the new product offering of such stores. Also added are children's play areas, entertainment centers, and maid services. To keep customers up-to-date on the new services—and loyal to the store—retailers have set up customer service clubs offering newsletters, invitations to events, and discounts, both in-store and at affiliated companies.[4]

Large retailers wish to offer a shopping experience to their consumers, and try to do so by providing luxury products, luxury services, and a luxurious environment. This increases the pressure for more diversity of products and services. Large retailers also attempt to give themes to their product offerings by regularly holding fairs that introduce or highlight specific product categories for a limited time.

Smaller retailers, in turn, see their main competitive niche in the area of convenience and in providing fresh products. In doing so, they are able to preserve a competitive advantage when compared to larger retailers, who cannot be as fully responsive in their delivery.

Notes

1. Randolph E. Ross, "Understanding the Japanese Distribution System: An Explanatory Framework," *European Journal of Marketing,* Vol. 17, No. 1, 1983, p. 12.

2. Mitsuaki Shimaguchi and Larry J. Rosenberg, "Demystifying Japanese Distribution," *Columbia Journal of World Business,* Spring 1979, p. 35.

3. "Softnomics: The Service-Oriented Economy of Japan," *JETRO, No. 35,* Tokyo, 1985, p. 2.

4. "The Depato: Inside Japan's Superstores," *Focus Japan,* November 1990, p. 3.

C H A P T E R

18

The Role of Distribution Information and Technology

A major revolution is also occurring in the information-processing area within the distribution system. Already in 1984, a MITI representative noted:

> The distribution industry is being increasingly required to more effectively meet consumer needs in a maturing industrial society. It must serve not only as a pipeline through which goods flow from producers to consumers, but also as a relay point allowing information to flow between the two. The information function of the distribution industry is expected to increase as the advanced information society develops. In other words, the importance of the distribution industry as a relay point for the flow of producer-consumer information will increase as the Japanese economy matures and handles more information.[1]

Five years later, MITI is even more adamant. The Director of the Commerce Policy Division in the Industrial Policy Bureau stated:

To meet the growing diversification and shorter cycle of consumer preferences, the distribution industry must introduce speedy and low-cost merchandise control and accurate control of customer data to be utilized in the development and marketing of new products. Efficiency through information management has now become indispensable for the distribution industry.[2]

The progress of this anticipated and urged information revolution is apparent, when one sees that the distribution industry in Japan currently accounts for 45 percent of computers used in all industries, while manufacturers and service industries utilize only 25 percent and 16 percent respectively.[3]

Technology penetration of the distribution sector is most visible in the employment of the POS (point of sale) system by channel members. Even though the system, labeled UPS, was initiated in the United States, Japan today boasts its largest acceptance. More than 43,000 stores use over 120,000 POS scanners.[4]

This computerized scanning system collects data on all the items carried and sold in the store. The resulting information assists in the control of sales and inventory, but is also used on an ongoing basis for research, merchandising, and planning purposes. Of equal importance is the use of the POS system in forging distribution information linkages between retailers, wholesalers, and manufacturers. The exchange of information between these channel members is progressing rapidly and assists in the development of a logistics system that transcends the narrow confines of the firm and optimizes the performance of the entire channel. As a result, major further improvements in channel management can be expected, due to a better ability to plan and be responsive to market needs.

Stores also encourage consumers to use store-issued credit cards or debit cards when paying for purchases. Since these cards are encoded with socioeconomic customer data, the POS system can greatly assist in customer segmentation, and provide a buying-habit analysis down to the time of day products are purchased, size of product package, and the impact of changes in day temperature. Other than in the United States and many European nations, privacy laws do not restrict such information accumulation, analysis or the sharing of the results between affiliated firms.

Additional uses of the POS system are for customer traffic analysis and merchandise layout. The system also permits many routine operations to be carried out automatically, including the output of the warehouse picking list based on the order data, additional order placing to the manufacturer through the inventory control system, issuing of invoices and price tags, and designation of the distribution route.[5] In addition, users benefit from more precise demand forecasting, a reduction in cash register errors and better personnel utilization.

The main purpose of the POS system is, however, not to reduce the number of employees. As one Japanese executive noted: "In the U.S., use of software in supermarkets is made because of 'hard' merits such as savings in labor cost. In Japan, we focus more on the 'soft' merits of these innovations such as the use of data for decision-making or for consumer satisfaction." Stores using the system have been able to reduce the number of checkout lanes by up to 20 percent; the freed-up employees are now used to foster more direct contact with customers. More service than before is now provided to customers in areas such as information about merchandise location and product usage. Apart from resulting in more informed and, it is hoped, more content customers, stores expect this increased service orientation to ease the introduction of new products, enhance product differentiation, and perhaps enable an increasing shift in the product mix toward products with high explanatory needs.

New Distribution Technology

Substantial changes are also taking place in physical distribution technology. A prime example is a Tokyo Seiyu store, which is part of the Seibu Group. This prototype store was opened as a result of the finding that, in conventional retail stores, 60 percent of employee time was devoted to the transport of merchandise, 20 percent to clerical and administrative work, and only 20 percent to human interaction. The store is designed to demonstrate the fusion of people and science, by having humans deal mainly with creative issues and services, and machines with the picking, holding, and transporting of products. Apart from offering features such as completely automated slicing and packaging of meat products, new systems for building and cleanliness control, and the use of experimental products, the store has completely automated its physical distribution function. Delivery trucks are parked by the driver and the doors are opened. Crates and pallets are automatically unloaded and transported to the store-attached warehouse, where a fully automated storage system is in place. Sales data are collected from the store through the POS system and are fed into the warehouse system, which in turn carries out the picking function in preparation for restocking. After the store closes, merchandise is automatically retrieved from the warehouse and restocked on the store's shelves. Concurrently, replenishment orders are placed with suppliers.

The system has problems with merchandise that is not bar-coded or source marked, but is operative and provides valuable information to the parent company. Seibu, in turn, plans to use the lessons learned from this new technology application to improve its own stores. It also plans to develop a consulting package for sale of the system to other stores.

All these technological developments may well mark a new era in distribution. As one U.S. executive noted:

Time was when the stream of visitors to supermarkets was one-way, from Japan to the U.S. The Seiyu store may signal a change of direction. More Americans may be packing their bags—along with their Japanese-made cameras and tape recorders—and head west across the Pacific. When Horace Greeley said, 'Go West, young man,' he never dreamed of the implications.[6]

Notes

1   Konaga, op. cit., p. 1.

2. Takashi Nakanomyo, "Distributors Use Information Management to Define Consumer Demands," *Business Japan,* October 1989, p. 44.

3. Ibid.

4. Ryosuko Asano, "Networks Raise Efficiency of Distribution Information Systems," *Business Japan,* October 1989, pp. 45–51.

5   Takashi Nakanomyo, op. cit., p. 44.

6. Robert O'Neill, "Go West Young Man—To Japan?" *Progressive Grocer,* January 1984, p. 10.

PART V

Entering the Market

C H A P T E R

19

Alternative Routes

As for all markets, there are various points of entry and various methods of getting into Japan. They are not very different in nature there, but the choice one makes may be quite different because, as noted, there are certain difficulties and complexities that must be considered. It is not enough just to go in, set up and staff a company, and then carry on as in more liberal economies like the United States and parts of Europe. And it really is essential to know the other players, especially those that belong to influential groupings.

These alternatives can best be graded according to the amount of effort on the part of the foreign company and the degree to which the effort is carried by a local partner.

The simplest approach is merely to seek a Japanese trading company or importer to receive and market the goods on your behalf. Or goods can be produced and marketed under license or the business franchised. This category makes the least demands, requires the least local knowledge, and is also the cheapest and fastest for the foreign company. While the risks and costs are relatively modest, the rewards are also proportionately smaller.

At the next level, the foreign company enters the Japanese market itself but does so with a Japanese partner. The partner may handle just distribution or production as well. The joint venture can be adjusted in keeping with each partner's share of activity, with the foreign company having a minority, equal or majority stake. This alternative naturally involves greater inputs in terms of finance, personnel, marketing and production knowhow. But at least the local partner can be counted on to handle those aspects it knows best and may be harder for an outsider in return for a share in the eventual rewards.

Many companies may prefer going it alone, setting up a local branch or subsidiary, staffing it, handling distribution, production, perhaps even R&D. This path was often blocked in earlier years, when tight regulations and strong administrative guidance directed foreign companies toward the preferred joint venture, with the foreign partner preferably holding 50 percent or less. Such arrangements are no longer imposed. But the daunting problems of running a wholly-owned venture remain. They must, therefore, be compensated by superior returns to justify this method, which can be achieved organically by growing a company, or through acquisition of an existing local entity.

The choice of level depends on many factors. One set is familiar to any company entering any market, namely the imperatives of selling and/or manufacturing a given product (or service). Much will depend on whether the product (or service) is sold to consumers or other companies, whether it is relatively small and/or inexpensive or large and/or expensive, whether it is top-of-the-line or quite ordinary, whether it requires considerable after-sales service, and so on. Thus, a preliminary step is to have the product carefully examined and perhaps tested on the Japanese market to see whether it will sell, who might buy it, which channels should be used to distribute it, etc.

It may transpire that the product chosen is not appropriate or could only be sold in such small quantities that there is no point in doing more than exporting, licensing, or franchising. If the prospects are greater, and the rewards sufficiently enticing, a joint venture or wholly owned company may seem justified. If, for some reason, one particular product (or service) does not succeed, this does not mean that others cannot do better. Changing the product (or service) rather than changing the point of entry may be the right response.

When picking products, there is a bit of folk wisdom which, while extremely widespread and repeatedly proffered, should be ignored. That is the notion that the Japanese are such demanding customers that only something truly unique or truly superior stands a chance. Certainly, such products stand a better chance per se. But other, quite ordinary ones can also do quite well if they offer notable differences in design, simpler operation, greater durability, or some other virtue. They can also benefit from the mere fact that they are "Western" and thus "different." Most important, they can sell on price. Japanese also buy goods because they are cheaper, especially if these are just standard goods that do not contribute to status or "face."

No less important, but considerably less familiar to foreign businessmen, it is necessary to consider the competitive situation and the other players. There are products (and whole sectors) where certain companies or groups truly dominate and there is little chance of foreigners achieving significant results. There are others that are relatively wide open, and foreign companies can join in with others. In addition, should an importer, distributor, or joint venture be sought, it must be considered which groups already have—or do not have—a member handling that product. This determines both whether partners are still available and which ones would be most suitable.

Finally, the point at which one enters is very much a function of commitment. Some companies are simply not willing or do not have the personnel and financial backing to do more than export, license, or franchise. Forming a joint venture, which should in principle last for a considerable time and will definitely make greater demands on limited resources, is a big step further. But at least the costs are shared, and a Japanese partner can handle the more complicated aspects. It takes very substantial commitment to go it alone in Japan. This is particularly true since it may take years before there is any return on the investment and more years to speak of a true success.

Given the complexities of the market and the need to know who is who among the players, many foreign businessmen lean heavily on the views of a consulting firm. It usually studies the product and market and suggests possible partners. It then acts as go-between to work out relations with Japanese importers, distributors, or manufacturers. While the consultant's advice may be indispensable and invaluable, it should never be forgotten that the consultant also has its own interests. It tends to prefer exporting, licensing, and franchising or a joint venture because it can continue providing advice (for a fee), whereas a wholly-owned company may soon dispense with its services. It may also have its own preferences among Japanese partners, recommending those it is more familiar with or which may offer some return.

While there are different ways of getting in and different degrees of commitment, they are not necessarily immutable. It may turn out that the product is doing well, that far more can be sold than had initially been supposed. Indeed, the demand may be such that local production becomes feasible. In addition to the first product, others may be added. There is, thus, no reason that the ladder cannot be mounted, advancing from mere exporting to a joint venture for marketing and perhaps production, and eventually even a wholly owned operation. That progression has occurred frequently.

It can also turn out that the first product did not do well, nor did any other. Or the importer did not perform well, the licensee accomplished little, and the franchisee was unsuccessful. Perhaps the joint venture got into trouble because it had the wrong local partner, or the foreign partner did not know how to deal with him, or a joint venture was just not the right path. Even a wholly-owned venture, one patiently nurtured over years, may not make a profit. It is still possible to change, either by getting other importers, licensees, or franchisees, seeking another partner, or conceding that it is impossible to proceed without a partner. These alternatives should always be borne in mind.

It is also necessary to consider one last possibility, the likes of which will rarely be mentioned by a consultant, who wants to continue earning fees, or other foreign companies, which hesitate to admit their own weaknesses. It may be appropriate just to withdraw. This is a terrible loss of "face" in Japan and within the foreign business community, and there is no doubt that it will be painful. But that is still preferable to wasting more funds, personnel, and time on an enterprise that simply does not click and will earn an even worse reputation.

Successes . . . and Failures

Using these various approaches, countless foreign companies have tried to crack the Japanese market. Many have succeeded, whether by exporting or setting up local operations. By 1989, there were nearly 3,000 foreign-affiliated companies and they were generating ever more revenue. A survey by the Ministry of International Trade and Industry showed that, in 1988, they accounted for some ¥10.4 trillion in sales or about one percent of sales by all corporations.[1] Over the years, according to the Ministry of Finance, they had invested some $15.6 billion, with the amount rising steadily. More than half of this investment came from the United States with Europe providing 20 percent, followed by Hong Kong and other Asian countries. Nearly 70 percent went into manufacturing, especially machinery and chemicals.[2]

So it is clearly possible to make a go of it. Moreover, despite the intrinsic difficulties, there has been a noticeable trend for companies to demonstrate greater commitment by setting up joint ventures or wholly-owned subsidiaries rather than merely exporting. More and more have also added local production facilities and sometimes R&D laboratories.

Many of the foreign-affiliated companies are regarded as a "success." It is pointed out that they are number one in some sectors, Coca Cola for soft drinks, McDonald's for fast foods, Schick for wet razors, Braun for electric razors, Nestlé for instant coffee, etc. IBM Japan is repeatedly cited as a high tech manufacturer that did extremely well and Citibank has been added in finance. Further winners are shown in Table 19-1.

Not only that, according to MITI, profits have been considerably higher than for Japanese companies, and this was confirmed by the American Chamber of Commerce in Japan and the European Business Community.[3]

But this "success" should not be exaggerated. Foreign companies are often leaders in very narrow segments. Their profits are good, but one must still consider the losses of earlier years. In addition, profit is not what motivates Japanese companies. They seek market share, and it must be admitted that even eminent foreign firms have lost market share. This includes IBM for computers, Xerox for

Table 19-1
Successful Foreign Companies in Japan

COUNTRY	FOREIGN COMPANY OR BRAND	PRODUCT
U.S.A.	Schick	Razors
	Polaroid	Instant cameras
	Coca-Cola	Soft drinks
	Johnson & Johnson	Adhesive tape
	IBM	Computers
	Del Monte	Tomato juice
	Johnson	Wax
	Pampers	Disposable diapers
	Kodak	Film
	Levis	Jeans
Germany	Braun	Electric razors
	Beiersdorf	Skin care cream
	BMW	Automobiles
	Karl Zeiss	Optical equipment
	Melita	Coffee maker products
	Puma	Exercise shoes
	Wella	Shampoo and hair care products
France	Louis Vuitton	Handbags or luggage
	Remy Martin	Liquor
	Fauchon	Jam, tea
U.K.	Lux	Soap
	Berry Brothers & Rudd	Scotch whisky
	Lipton	Tea
	Twinings	Tea
Switzerland	Nestlé	Instant coffee
Denmark	Lego	Construction toys
Italy	Olivetti	Typewriters
	Fila	Sportswear

SOURCE: *Quick Reference on Japan-U.S. Trade* and *Quick Reference on Japan-EC Economic Relations*, JETRO.

photocopiers, Procter and Gamble for disposable diapers, Johnson & Johnson for Band Aids and many more.

Nor should it be forgotten that there have also been losers in what is manifestly a very tough market, the toughest that most companies will find among the liberal economies. According to one consulting firm, the failure rate of Western businesses in Japan may run as high as 50 percent.[4] Failure is most prevalent among relatively small firms that cannot muster the time and money needed to penetrate the market. This applies particularly to ordinary ones, which do not possess special products or technologies and, more generally, those from less advanced countries. But even some of the biggest American multinationals have failed. Of the Fortune 500, only about 200 actually have local operations in Japan, while another 100 have technical tie-ups. About 200 have attempted to enter the market but failed.[5]

Most significantly, it is not because they ignored the importance of Japan or failed to make reasonable efforts. According to an exhaustive study by the United States International Trade Commission:

> There are volumes of anecdotal evidence about U.S. companies that have "done all the right things" to distribute their products in Japan—developed products of equal or superior quality to Japanese products that are suitable for Japanese consumers, developed a long-term market strategy by obtaining information on consumer trends, developed effective advertising, after sales plans, and sales promotion campaigns and shown a long-term commitment to the market. For some reason, despite a major commitment of time and resources, even well-known companies with large market shares in other countries have been unable to either enter Japan's distribution channels or to distribute their products at competitive prices.[6]

Notes

1. Ministry of International Trade and Industry, *Gaishikei kigyo no doko (Trends in Foreign-Affiliated Companies)*, 1989.

2. Ministry of Finance.

3. MITI, op. cit.

4. A.T. Kearney Management Consultants, "Winning Operating Strategies in Japan," 1989, p. 3.

5. United States International Trade Commission, *Japan's Distribution System and Options for Improving U.S. Access*, June 1990, p. 6.

6. Ibid., pp. 6-7.

20

Exporting, Licensing and Franchising

Many foreign companies, either because they do not operate on a large enough scale or find that access to the Japanese market is difficult, prefer limiting themselves to exporting. Others will license their knowhow to Japanese companies that produce the article locally and then market it. Franchising may also be undertaken through a local partner rather than establishing a direct presence in Japan and allocating franchises on one's own. This shows a lesser degree of commitment to the Japanese market, but is certainly a valid approach for some products or sectors or in the initial stage of doing business.

Theoretical Considerations

As any foreign businessman who has tried will know, it is not that simple to pick the right Japanese importer, licensee, or franchisee. There are the ordinary complications of deciding whether the agent is well-managed, financially sound, competent, and has the right approach and will to succeed. There are also aspects that are somewhat more peculiar to the Japanese situation.

147

First, it must be remembered that the importer or partner can vary considerably in nature. Most are primarily traders; they are in the business of importing (and often also exporting). This is what they live from and know best. But many are also either manufacturers or closely related to manufacturers. As noted, manufacturers in certain sectors have their own network of outlets. And traders, while not actually producing goods, may well be exporting them for related firms. Only retailers are purely commercial entities, although now some produce "own brand" articles as well.

Second, it is necessary to consider the size and scope of these intermediaries, which vary enormously. There are some 10,000 trading companies, but only nine of them qualify as general trading companies (*sogo shosha*). They are widely diversified, active in numerous sectors, mobilizing huge staffs and tremendous resources. These traders are so large that, collectively, they account for as much as three-quarters of Japan's imports and a fifth of its wholesaling volume. The big nine, in order of turnover, are C. Itoh, Mitsui, Marubeni, Mitsubishi, Sumitomo, Nissho Iwai, Toyo Menka, Nichimen, and Kanematsu-Gosho.[1]

Aside from them, there are countless smaller traders (*senmon shosha*) whose range of activities and size is considerably less. In addition, they are much more specialized, handling a narrower array of articles in some few sectors. Many of them are part of wholesalers which, along with domestic operations, have added imported goods. There are infinitely more retailers, but the only ones that engage in much (and increasingly more) importing are about a dozen supermarket chains (*supa*) and two dozen department store chains (*depato*).

The third consideration, more subtle but no less significant, is the relationship between the importer and other local companies. For most importers have connections that influence their effectiveness or lack thereof as a means of access to Japan. Many are part of a *keiretsu* or horizontal grouping, including the *sogo shosha* that are core members.[2] Others depend heavily on manufacturers and their vertical groupings. And major retailers tend to set up informal groupings of their own. Only the smaller traders and foreign firms remain relatively independent.

This means it is not that simple to pick the ideal partner, and sufficient time and attention should be devoted to this task. Some of the crucial parameters follow.

Probably the easiest question is whether to use a large trader or one of the smaller ones. The answer is frequently supplied by the *sogo shosha* themselves. They are eminently suitable vehicles for products that have a fairly large market and can be handled on a large scale. This includes most raw materials, bulk commodities, heavy machinery and capital goods, and big ticket items like aircraft or satellites. They are less adapted to handling smaller, cheaper consumer articles, especially those that require considerable after-sales service, such as electronics, household appliances, garments, or foods and beverages. And they are not adequately specialized for many machine tools, metal and woodworking equipment, etc. For these, smaller traders are often more appropriate.

The next question, whose answer seems self-evident at first, is considerably trickier. Should one use an importer that is already specialized in the sector or one that is only marginally involved or outside? The advantages of the specialized firm are obvious: it already knows the sector, can handle the product more readily, has existing distribution channels and trained personnel. But, if it is already in that sector, it probably also handles competing products or (if it is a manufacturer) makes them itself. This means it is less likely to make a serious effort for imported goods that could cut into the sales of its own line.

The third question, the hardest to grapple with, is what to do about intercompany relationships. If the importer does have a relationship with a *keiretsu*, it has easier access to the other group members and can push sales more effectively with them. On the other hand, it will be less effective in dealing with other groups, and thus an independent agent, one with equal access to all (but admittedly privileged access to none) may be better in the long run. As for companies that have vertical sales groupings, the outlets are already there. But they will not be used aggressively for competing products. Thus, such importers should handle only niche products or goods that are somewhat different and round out their range.

When it comes to licensing, the situation is much more straightforward. It is really possible to work effectively only with another manufacturer, one that is in the same or a closely-related sector, because only it will have the production knowhow and facilities. But it is still necessary to choose carefully, again avoiding those that either produce the same or similar articles or have close relations with other manufacturers with competing goods. Once again, it is best to have them handle niche goods or products that supplement their existing range.

For franchising, since this most often involves services and softer technologies, it would again seem advantageous to cooperate with a partner in the same or similar sector or at least in the service industry. This increasingly includes the *sogo shosha* that have recently made an effort to expand into services as sales of older imports slacken. They may also have subsidiaries that produce the necessary raw materials. And, of course, they have access to the financial resources many franchises need to get started. Retailers, with existing outlets where franchises can be located or the land and property to open them, are also interesting.

From this discussion, it is obvious that there can be definite advantages to working through an importer, licensee, or franchisee. It knows the market better and can be more effective in selling the product or service. It already has offices, warehouses, and other facilities; it employs qualified personnel and it has access to distribution channels. In fact, it will be making the major effort in Japan for whatever margin it can obtain.

But there are also drawbacks. By working through an intermediary, it is hard to know just how vigorously and effectively it is selling, whether sales are at an acceptable level or could be raised by a more dedicated effort. There is little or no control over how the product is distributed, displayed, advertised, and so on. And there is even less feedback from the customers. There is also less knowledge of the competitors, how their products differ, whether they are better or worse, cheaper or more expensive, and, above all, whether they are gaining market share. For licensing and franchising, there is a risk that instructions will not be followed strictly and quality may be ignored.

Pricing can be a particularly sensitive issue, especially in Japan. There is a tendency to work through a sole agent which, in return for exclusive rights, should make a commensurate effort. But it can choose to sell to a more select public at a higher price or apply a lower one for the mass market. It is usually easier to take the former approach, and many foreign products, almost by dint of being Western, are categorized as *hakuraihin* and treated as luxuries of a sort. That is fine for the importer. It can sell proportionately less and still make decent profits. But selling fewer units hurts the producer. It also loses out if the price is so high as to attract parallel imports or local competitors.[3]

Practical Examples

As noted, there is a broad array of alternatives, and different ones have been chosen by different foreign entrants.

It is understandable that producers of commodities and raw materials have stuck to the *sogo shosha*, which often set up special divisions or subsidiaries for agricultural produce, timber, mineral ores (coal, iron, bauxite, etc.) and sometimes petroleum. In so doing, they often use the group trader of related steelmakers, aluminum and copper refiners, petrochemical producers, and so forth. The *sogo shosha* loomed large in aerospace, Nichimen acting as general agent for Airbus Industries and C. Itoh handling satellites of Hughes Aircraft. Some distributed automobiles (Nissho Iwai for Ford), and several now handle imported cigarettes (Mitsui for Philip Morris and Mitsubishi for R.J. Reynolds). Itoman is still a big textile and garment importer, while Nissho Iwai expanded into foodstuffs. They have also been involved in franchising of late, with Mitsubishi joining Kentucky Fried Chicken and Nissho Iwai, David's Cookies.

But the smaller traders have been no less active, each in its respective field. They have cornered much of the imports of garments, especially high fashion articles, machinery and machine tools, household appliances, books, furniture, and so on. They have taken a clean sweep of specialized areas like pharmaceuticals and medical equipment. Initially, most automobiles were distributed by specialized firms, the largest being Yanase. But many foreign companies have preferred using foreign importers like Dodwell, Jardine, Caldbeck-MacGregor, or Denmark's East Asiatic, especially for upmarket products including foods, beverages, and fashion goods. Dodwell, for example, represents Brinton carpets,

Christie's contemporary prints, and Mars pet food, as well as Pitney-Bowes office machinery.

Retailers have clearly increased their share of imports over recent years. They have been importing ordinary clothing, furniture, household appliances, gift items and fashion goods in steadily growing amounts. Most of this comes from Europe. But there is also keen interest in articles from East and Southeast Asia, which are sold on price rather than quality. Thus, Daiei began selling video tape recorders made by Korea's Samsung, and a small chain of "NIE Stores" devoted exclusively to such imports was launched.

One of the more interesting innovations is the "shop-in-the-shop," where foreign producers directly or through an import agent sell their wares in return for a percentage of the sales. Such shops exist for Hermes clothing in Seibu and Royal Doulton china in Mitsukoshi. There is hardly a fashion designer or luxury-good maker that does not have a shop somewhere in Tokyo by now.

Not surprisingly, parts and components suppliers have had the hardest time penetrating the market. In order to do so, they have to comply with Japanese standards, guarantee good quality, and open warehouses so that items can be delivered when needed. This only made sense once a fairly large and steady stream of orders could be expected. Among those that broke through were Bendix, which became a disc brake pad supplier of Toyota; Goodyear, which provided tires for exported cars and finally some of Toyota's domestic models; Spirax Sarco Ltd., which specializes in steam valves; and OSRAM (a subsidiary of Siemens), which became the leading supplier of automobile head light halogen lamps. In order to be more than a niche supplier, it was plainly necessary to offer something special as for OSRAM's lamps.

On the whole, licensing was undertaken with another manufacturer. Corning initially licensed its technology to Asahi Glass and, more recently, Volkswagen agreed to have some models assembled by Nissan. Given the tight links between automakers and suppliers, many auto parts are produced under license. The same applies for some special electronics products. And the bulk of the fashion goods, while sporting the names of foreign designers, are actually produced under license in Japan. One among many is the arrangement between Ralph Lauren and Seibu.

For franchising, there has been a veritable boom with well over a hundred foreign chains involved including McDonald's, Kentucky Fried Chicken, Baskin-Robbins, Mr. Donut and Family Mart, among others. Yet, while the names and logos are foreign, the actual operation is usually handled by a Japanese firm. The local partners in the forementioned cases are Mitsubishi, Fujita, Fujiya, Duskin and Seibu, a mixture of trading companies, manufacturers, and retailers.

Foreign companies have usually chosen to work with importers or manufacturers in the same sector. This is not surprising. But it was not always the case. For example, while most automakers sold through Yanase or another automaker, Volvo initially chose Teijin, a textile company, as its agent. While Baskin-Robbins set up shop with Fujiya, a confectioner, and 7-Eleven tied up with Ito Yokado, a big retailer, Mr. Donut selected Duskin, originally a cleaning equipment leasing company. Whirlpool sold refrigerators through Sony, and Apple Computer used Canon as its distributor. Quite often, products sold through similar companies were themselves distinctive, such as the Scotch whiskies or foreign-brand beers imported by local brewers, or specialty foods handled by local foodstuff producers.

It is hard to tell how successful any of these operations were, since neither party went out of its way to reveal dissatisfaction, while proudly acclaiming any supposed success. Still, there is no doubt that some foreign companies were unhappy with their importer, licensee, or franchising partner. And complaints of "overpromising" (i.e. promising to do more than ever materialized) by big traders and sole agents were distressingly widespread. In some cases, the foreign party simply withdrew, in others, it changed partners.

Even more symptomatic has been the tendency for relatively successful companies to move up to a higher level of commitment. This usually meant, while still using the same importer, licensee or franchisee, to set up a permanent office in Japan to follow sales more closely, obtain some feedback from customers, and generate more advertising. Or, in fewer cases, it meant handling distribution directly, either through the same firms that had been selling all along or new ones, whether independent or controlled.

There are numerous examples of this, more of which will be mentioned later. They include virtually all the major pharmaceutical companies, which quickly established a presence either through a joint venture or on their own. More recently, automakers have broken away from earlier importers and set up their own channels, BMW and Mercedes Benz being most notable.[4] In consumer goods, this time for top end products, Waterford Wedgwood stopped using its general import agency and went over to direct sales; Salomon Sports switched from local trading companies to direct sales; and Chanel now distributes nearly all its perfumes, cosmetics, clothes, and accessories directly. In industry, the trend was from licensing to direct production, with Corning working through Iwaki Glass. And Toys R Us wants to handle its own operations rather than licensing or franchising.

There have also been cases where foreign companies simply could not find importers to handle their goods or could not use existing distribution channels. Electrolux is one of the most intriguing. It has excellent household appliances, including vacuum cleaners that proved quite popular. But the electric appliance stores depended on local makers, so the Swedish multinational had to open its own network of door-to-door saleswomen.[5] It was only later that Sharp accepted to carry its goods. Others that chose door-to-door sales were Tupperware, Franklin Mint, and Amway. Meanwhile, the Sharper Image and Sears, Roebuck are trying direct mail. And MTS just went ahead and opened its own stores for Tower Records.

If the system had been more flexible and responsive, many of the switches and alternative channels would not have been necessary. If it had been more open, countless exporters who never cracked the market at all would have been able to sell to Japan.[6]

Notes

1. See Kunio Yoshihara, *Sogo Shosha* (Tokyo: Oxford University Press, 1982), and Alexander K. Young, *The Sogo Shosha* (Boulder: Westview Press, 1979).

2. See USITC, op. cit., pp. 30-40.

3. See Kenji Sanekata, "Sole Import Agents: More Harm Than Good? *Economic Eye*, Summer 1990, pp. 26-28.

4. "Japanese Car Market Continuing Up-Scale Drive," *Tokyo Business Today*, May 1990, pp. 50-53.

5. *Focus Japan*, November 1989, p. 9.

6. For further comments on the drawbacks of exporting, see Mark Zimmerman, *How to do Business with the Japanese* (New York: Random House, 1985), pp. 236-53.

C H A P T E R

21

Joint Ventures

Despite the ease and limited resources required for merely exporting, licensing, and franchising, this route often proves inadequate. As noted, key decisions regarding marketing, advertising, pricing, and so on are left to others, and there is little feedback. Also, these methods work best for relatively modest quantities. As sales grow or other articles are added, it may become appropriate, even essential, to take a step further. Thus, either for large companies with a broad array of products or those that have already achieved what they could through exporting, it may eventually be decided to set up an operation in Japan.

Theoretical Considerations

No matter how serious it is about this, in many cases, the foreign company does not want to go it alone. Its biggest lacks are adequate knowledge of distribution (or access to the right channels) and familiarity with local circumstances, and it often seeks a partner who can provide that in exchange for access to the product and technology. This is the basic tradeoff in most cooperative undertakings. But there are other significant aspects as well. If actual production will be launched, it is useful to have a partner that can share or provide factory capacity. Given the high cost of land and premises, this may also be sought. And, with the labor market less flexible, personnel may be another need.

Thus, joint ventures could be established that will naturally differ from case to case. This will depend on how the financial burden is shared as well as what each partner provides. While most foreign companies prefer having a majority, perhaps even a substantial majority, in Japan it frequently occurs that the local partner has to provide more than elsewhere (not only finance but land, facilities, personnel, distribution). In earlier years, a 50:50 split was most common and, due to regulations, hard to exceed until the liberalization of foreign investment in 1980. The share nowadays varies much more, with the foreign partner able to obtain whatever the local partner concedes.

As for exporting, a crucial decision is which local partner to tie up with. The various considerations enumerated for exporting still apply. The size of the partner is important since many larger Japanese firms will not bother with smaller foreign ones unless there is a special interest. It is necessary to decide which group to tie up with or whether to stand aside. Specialized companies have advantages, but those may be eclipsed if they, or related firms, are direct competitors.

It is also indispensable to consider what the actual function of the joint venture is, simply to market better or also to produce locally. In the former case, the earlier trading company or specialized importer may be kept on as joint venture partner if it was effective. If the aim is to expand distribution, then another, more promising distributor may be chosen—or none, leaving the new local venture greater leeway to use several channels. If manufacturing is also involved, then the partner must have the capability. In some cases, as when opening retail outlets or automobile distributorships, the availability of land can be a primary concern.

While all these factors are important, it has often turned out for joint ventures that nothing was more fateful than deciding whether to tie up with a company in the same sector or an outsider. The natural tendency is to take the former. Such a partner obviously understands the products, can more readily manufacture them, has better access to distribution, and employs suitably trained personnel. The joint venture could, therefore, get off to a faster and smoother start.

However, in the longer run, there is a much greater danger. The foreign company provides the product and/or technology. This is ordinarily a superior product or technology but, nonetheless, one that can be learned by the local partner in the course of business and perhaps also improved upon. If it is sufficiently capable, and this is true of most Japanese manufacturers, the local partner could ultimately come up with an alternative product that it might push more eagerly than that of the joint venture. That would obviously detract from its benefits.

If, for one reason or another, the parties were to fall out, this would not be so disastrous for the local partner. It already has a major operation of its own; it now has a familiarity with the new product and could replace it with another import or fashion its own. The foreign partner still has its original product, but it does not have the distribution channels to sell it. It may be left without a local factory in which to produce or even the land and premises in which to operate. Worse, it does not have the essential personnel.

This last point, which is far more significant in Japan than elsewhere, must be expanded upon. Japan's employment system is based largely on "lifetime" employment, with staff built up over the years as new classes of employees are recruited from school. There is a relatively small floating labor force that can be hired by any comer. And thus it is hard, costly, and time consuming for a fledgling company to recruit personnel. It is usually much easier just to "borrow" staff from the Japanese partner. But these employees owe much greater loyalty to that partner, may indeed be part-and-parcel of its workforce. In the event of a breakup, most would go back to the Japanese partner and the foreign partner would thus not only forfeit the staff but the experience they have acquired and contacts they have made.[1]

For this reason, foreign companies should seriously reflect on what would happen in the event of a breakup, even while they are first entering into a hopefully rewarding partnership. They must decide whether they really do want to tie up with a knowledgeable partner that could become a troublesome rival at a later date, or whether they would not prefer one that is just a distributor or maybe a manufacturer in a different sector. Whatever the conclusion, they must also decide just how advisable it is to depend on the local partner for land, premises, distribution, and, less obvious initially, personnel.

This, by the way, is not something that can simply be settled by giving the foreign partner a larger share of the ownership. Nor can it be written into the contract effectively. The Japanese partner usually does its best to be helpful, offering land, premises, personnel, etc., because this is the easier way. But it is perfectly aware that it also gains greater influence. A foreign partner that accepts the easy way out may find it has lost its ability to maneuver if ever the relations sour.

Practical Examples

There is no question that the joint venture has been the most frequently used method, and it remains popular even at present when it is no longer imposed by Japanese bureaucrats. It is the route adopted by most larger foreign companies who want to start off with a reasonably high profile and on a scale not really permitted by mere exporting. It is even more interesting to note just how many firms that started by exporting eventually entered into joint ventures, sometimes with the earlier importer.[2]

Joint ventures have been formed by dozens of major companies and multitudes of smaller ones. In some cases, they have actually set up several with different partners, such as DuPont with Toray and Mitsui for different chemical products.

They prevail in specialized areas where it is necessary to work closely with a partner rather than count on its ability to produce under license, which is why Corning set up Iwaki Glass. Such sectors include chemicals (the DuPont joint ventures, Sumitomo 3M, Musashino Geigy, etc.), computers and electronics (Honeywell-NEC, Yokogawa-Hewlett-Packard), and office machinery (Fuji Xerox). But no sector saw more emerge than pharmaceuticals (Bayer Yakuhin, Searle Yakuhin, Miles-Sankyo, Fujisawa-Astra, Bristol-Myers Lion, etc.).

They exist not only for hard products but soft ones and services. Thus there were tie-ups between CBS and Sony and EMI and Toshiba for records, Seagram and Kirin and Allied-Lyons and Suntory for beverages, General Foods and Ajinomoto and Borden and Meiji for foodstuffs, McGraw-Hill and Nikkei for publishing, Moore and Toppan for printing, and McCann-Erickson and Hakuhodo for advertising. Most of the franchises were also run under joint ventures, McDonald's with Mitsubishi, Kentucky Fried Chicken with Fujita, to name just two. One interesting wrinkle was the decision of Toys R Us to join up with McDonald's rather than a purely Japanese partner.

In some of these cases, it was like with like. Caterpillar joined Mitsubishi to build construction machinery in the same way as chemical firms joined chemical firms or drug companies joined drug companies in the examples listed above. But there were frequently gaps that the foreign partner filled: Xerox adding photocopy machines, General Foods offering Maxwell House coffee, McGraw-Hill bringing its string of publications, and McCann-Erickson and Hakuhodo teaming up to provide American customers with advertising in Japan and Japanese customers with the same in America.

Still, there were some cases where the foreign entrant clearly chose a partner in another sector. The most noteworthy was the tie-up between Warner Lambert and K. Hattori, where Schick's sales were entrusted not to a razor maker or distributor but the producer of Seiko watches, which built up new and highly effective channels. Reebok tied up with Okamoto Industries, which produced rubber and plastic articles but not high-fashion sports shoes. Ralston Purina picked Taiyo Fishery as its partner in a pet foods joint venture. And, even more remote, Allstate Life Insurance joined with Seibu, which sold policies through it retail outlets.

Most of the joint ventures were fairly successful. But not all.[3] That much is obvious from the fact that some foreign forms ultimately withdrew (or were bought out by their partner). Particularly notable cases involved Dow Chemical and Asahi Chemical, International Harvester and Komatsu, RJR Nabisco and Yamazaki Bakery, Borden and Meiji, and Ralston Purina and Taiyo Fishery. Other major divestments include ICI, Phillips Petroleum, GTE, Kimberly Clark, Everready (Union Carbide) and Hercules.[4] Even more intriguing are cases where foreign-affiliated companies (or their foreign owners) were bought up by the Japanese, such as Shaklee, 7-Eleven, and CBS.

Just which partner has benefited most from any joint venture is rather hard to determine since disappointment is clearly expressed only when joint ventures actually come apart—if then. But there is no doubt that clever Japanese companies squeezed everything they could from any technology transfer and often got into a position where they could do without the foreign partner or its products. This was most noticeable for computers and electronics, machinery and machine tools, chemicals and foods and beverages. Nothing was more striking than the pharmaceutical sector, where firms that had once been mere distributors quickly became manufacturers with their own line of drugs.

Notes

1. For the significance of this factor, and ways to overcome or avoid difficulties, see Vladimir Puck, "Joint Ventures with the Japanese, the Key Role of HRM," *Euro-Asia Business Review*, October 1987, pp. 38-39.

2. For an insider's view of joint ventures, see Zimmerman, op. cit., pp. 218-35.

3. See Abegglen and Stalk, op. cit., pp. 226-31, and "Successes and Failures of Foreign Firms in Japan," *Oriental Economist*, June 1985, pp. 8-14.

4. *Tokyo Business Today*, April 1989, p. 6.

C H A P T E R

Wholly-Owned Ventures

While exporting and joint ventures are easier routes, they manifestly have draw-backs. The most important ones cited so far are inefficient marketing, limited feedback from clients, inadequate loyalty of personnel, and shared profits. But perhaps the worst disadvantage is simply lack of control. In the words of Frank Downing, president of SmithKline Beecham Japan, "With joint marketing or partners or whatever, you're not in control."[1]

Theoretical Considerations

Since many foreign managers expected to encounter such difficulties or actually faced them in earlier attempts, they decided to opt for a wholly owned company. This is particularly appropriate for multinationals, which have more experience of running operations abroad as well as the financial and personnel backing to get one started. It is also suitable for those with a broad range of products that can be handled in various ways with different distribution channels and/or local partners. When companies have special knowhow or proprietary technologies they do not want to divulge, they naturally think of 100 percent ownership. And many quite simply refuse to share control or have a tradition of going it alone.

161

In more and more cases, the foreign company simply outgrew any earlier arrangements and realized the need to take charge if it wanted to reach its full potential. This means that 100 percent ownership is often an outgrowth of success in the Japanese market. It makes it possible to tap a broader range of distribution channels, apply different production methods, and cooperate with more local partners. Control also makes it much easier to move into local production or engage in research and development.

However, having cited the advantages of running your own show, it is necessary to remember that there are added costs and problems as well. Little need be said about the sheer cost of buying land, renting or building premises, covering the cost of utilities and telecommunications, and buying advertising in one of the most expensive places in the world. That is obvious enough. What is less visible, at first, is that going it alone means you do not have the support of local partners and may find other firms regard you as more of a competitor than before.

But the biggest headache usually turns out to be the need to recruit personnel. As indicated above, Japanese-style management makes it harder to obtain staff from an open labor market. Most qualified personnel are already working for some other company, and few can be hired on short notice. This means that either less adequate staff must be accepted or it is necessary to use headhunters and wean staff away from competitors. What happens all too often is that foreign firms bid employees away from one another as opposed to rival Japanese companies, and this personnel, whatever its qualifications otherwise, may be less capable and loyal. It is also considerably more expensive and has come to expect more free time and perks.

The alternative is to do as the Japanese do, namely recruit youngsters fresh out of high school or college. But even that is easier said than done. Most schools already have connections with Japanese companies to whom they traditionally recommend the best candidates, and they may have few or none left over for a foreign company. A foreign company, in addition, entices fewer Japanese who ordinarily seek a safer career with a large Japanese company. Those who come may well have more imagination and initiative but perhaps less discipline. Even if this method is applied and perfected, it would take several decades to have a staff that has been entirely recruited and trained in-house.

Practical Examples

While there is a fairly large number of wholly-owned companies in Japan, they are far fewer than might be expected and still only represent a minority. That is because, until the 1980s, it was rather hard to obtain 100 percent ownership because of various regulations and restrictions or bureaucratic interference.[2] In fact, during the first postwar decades, it was almost impossible to establish a wholly-owned operation unless the company had been active in Japan prior to the war or offered what was regarded as a "strategic" product. Then it might be able to negotiate from a position of strength.

Since the amendment of the investment laws in 1980, however, it has become much simpler to have 100 percent control, and this is increasingly common, although still only accounting for about a fifth of all foreign-affiliated companies. The route is taken both by new entrants that want to go it alone and older ones that have decided to adapt or shed earlier joint ventures. Often, the foreign company will set up a wholly-owned operation that merely coordinates any existing distribution and production arrangements, but it may also replace them with its own. Whatever the reason and modus operandi, it is obvious that 100 percent is increasingly preferred to 50 percent.

One of the oldest, and certainly the best known, is IBM Japan. But there are many other high-tech firms in this category, including Motorola, Texas Instruments, Intel and Apple Computers. Other companies with unique products or proprietary technologies are Polaroid, Eastman Kodak, and Tetra Pak as well as Nestlé (instant coffee) and Coca Cola. Some of the oil companies (Mobil, Esso) and some of the automakers (BMW, Mercedes Benz) also have wholly-owned subsidiaries. In the financial sector, this is the case for nearly all the banks, securities houses and insurance companies.

While many companies started out with 100 percent ownership, others sought it after earlier experiences of joint ownership. Campbell Soup is a good example. Others which have achieved or are working toward 100 percent are TRW, GE, and Hewlett-Packard. The most intriguing sector is pharmaceuticals, where just about every foreign entrant seems to be boosting its share of the ownership or taking over outright—if it had not done so at the outset. This includes Sandoz, Merck, Pfizer, Schering-Plough, and especially Johnson & Johnson.

But the establishment of a wholly owned entity does not necessarily mean that the earlier cooperative arrangements were done away with. Often, this new company merely supplemented existing joint ventures and acted as the core of an emerging group. That is what happened with Bayer, BASF, DuPont, Exxon, General Electric, and Philips, each of which has a half-dozen or more firms in which it holds 20 percent or more. IBM Japan is naturally the most prominent example of such a group now that it has begun forming business tie-ups with Japanese partners.[3]

However it may be done, the transformation from a cooperative venture with Japanese partners to one in which the foreign company is clearly boss must be a gentle and tactful one, given the importance of human relations. A fine example of this is Lego, the Danish toy maker, which had been exporting to Japan since 1962 through an experienced toy distributor, Makoto Kato, who first discovered Lego at European toy fairs. This arrangement was satisfactory for some time since Japan was a remote and still smallish market. Then, in 1977, Lego decided to expand and take charge. Rather than drop Mr. Kato, he was made chairman of

Lego Japan, and his employees provided the initial staff for the new office. Chairman Kato then visited the various wholesalers and retailers to encourage them to keep working with Lego.[4]

Many of the wholly-owned ventures have gone into local manufacturing and have state-of-the-art facilities. Most prominent is obviously IBM, but this was also done by TI, Motorola, and others. Pharmaceutical firms are producing more of their own drugs than ever. Givaudan makes its own flavors and fragrances and Nestlé many of its foods. Rather than license, Levi produces most of its clothing in local factories, not owned by it but entirely dedicated to its production. Grace Japan makes it own sealants and polymers. And these are just a few examples of what is done in hundreds of foreign-run plants and factories.

More and more companies are also adding research and development capabilities, ones they would certainly not like to share with partners. In some cases, this could scarcely be avoided, as for pharmaceuticals, where local testing is required. But electronics firms and especially semiconductor makers must adapt products to clients' needs. Foodstuff producers also have to adjust to local tastes, and fashion designers tailor their clothing to fit the Japanese physique.

This earlier R & D effort is now expanding dramatically as firms try to benefit from highly-educated researchers in one of the world's most technologically advanced countries. That is why pharmaceutical firms are now opening special research centers, including Upjohn, Ciba-Geigy, Bristol Myers, Eli Lilly and Glaxo. IBM has several huge R & D facilities that occasionally upstage the home office. Recently, companies that had not even been particularly active in Japan realized the benefits of such research, including ICI and Eastman Kodak. By now there are over 200 foreign-owned R & D facilities.

These, however, are subsidiary reasons for setting up a wholly-owned venture. Judging by their actions, nothing is more essential than realigning the distribution system. It usually involves at least a closer scrutiny of the activities of existing distributors, perhaps weeding some out and adding new ones. It means increasing the establishment of your own marketing network alongside or instead of the former one. This has occurred with virtually every company mentioned thus far. And it is most noticeable again for pharmaceuticals, with Eli Lilly, Ciba-Geigy, Squibb, and Schering-Plough most noteworthy. There is also a major shakeup in automobile distribution, with many foreign makers choosing new partners or setting up their own distributorships, none more energetically than BMW.

Over the years, the wholly owned ventures have realized that they can become an effective part of the corporate community only by recruiting and promoting Japanese personnel. By now, the vast majority maintain expatriates only in top executive positions or as advisors, and some have already localized personnel 100 percent. Those that have been around longest have begun recruiting younger employees straight from school, although for older, mid-career staff, they are forced to draw from the floating pool of retired managers or those who have been poached from other companies, frequently foreign ones. While only IBM Japan is fully acclimatized, attracting eager graduates of the best colleges, employment in foreign-affiliated companies is becoming more acceptable.

Obviously, it is not enough just to recruit Japanese staff, they must be organized and treated differently from staff in the United States or Europe.[5] Thus, a modified Japanese management system has evolved, one combining a bit more initiative and incentives for more dynamic employees with a greater degree of job security and group activities. In addition, foreign-affiliated companies are adopting more and more Japanese practices with regard to advertising, distribution, quality control, pricing, and so on.[6] This is in keeping with the old adage revised to read: "When in Japan, do as the Japanese." But it results even more from the fact that foreign tactics have failed so often in Japan.

While it has been stated repeatedly, there is no harm in quoting yet another expatriate with extensive experience in Japan, Victor Harris, president of Max Factor K.K. "When all is said and done, it still remains true that anyone, in any business, who wants to be successful here must remember: Japan is as different a kind of marketplace as it is a culture and society. You have to do it *their* way or not at all."[7]

But it is best not to exaggerate. The Japanese way, no matter how good and effective, also has flaws. Moreover, no matter how hard foreigners try to copy Japanese techniques, they will never be as good at it as the Japanese. If they truly want to succeed in Japan, they must be one up on the Japanese. They must do something differently and, hopefully, also better. So it does not hurt to end with a quotation from a Japanese working for a foreign company, President Ikehata of Spaulding Japan, who believes that foreign companies should not feel overly bound by the need to "do as the Japanese." According to him, "You can't entirely ignore tradition. But don't get too hung up on customs. I'm a Japanese, but I realize that to do something new you can't just say, 'that's the way we've always done it.'"[8]

Notes

1. *Asian Wall Street Journal*, September 12, 1988, p. 10.

2. See Dan Fenno Henderson, op. cit., pp. 18-35.

3. Dodwell, *Industrial Groupings In Japan*, pp. 260-99.

4. *Financial Times*, July 9, 1990, p. III-I.

5. For more on personnel management, see Thomas J. Nevins, *Labor Pains and the Gaijin Boss - Hiring, Managing and Firing the Japanese* (Tokyo: Japan Times, 1984).

6. For more on how foreign companies are managed, see Jackson N. Huddleston, Jr., *Gaijin Kaisha, Running a Foreign Business in Japan* (Armonk: M.E. Sharpe, 1990).

7. *Japan Update*, Winter 1987, p. 25.

8. *Focus Japan*, March 1990, p. 8.

Acquisitions

While foreign companies can expand gradually, working their way up from exporting, to local marketing and then actual production, they may find the process excessively slow. In most other countries, the quicker alternative is acquisition. This is done quite regularly in the United States and Europe but not in Japan. Although Japanese companies have not hesitated to acquire American or European ones, usually through friendly but occasionally also hostile takeovers, there has been much less of this in Japan. For example, in 1989, in the midst of the takeover boom, Japanese companies swallowed up some $14 billion in American firms in contrast to less than $1 billion in Japanese assets for the U.S.[1] And they came away with some very big names like CBS and Firestone compared to relative small fry for the Americans.

Theoretical Considerations

The reasons for wanting to acquire local entities are somewhat different in Japan. Obtaining product knowhow or advanced technologies is less prevalent. That is partly because the only foreign firms large enough to attempt a takeover are usually also very advanced themselves. But it is even more so because large manufacturers are simply not up for sale and smaller ones tend to be more backward. The overriding concern is more often to improve the distribution network and control it more effectively. Foreign companies have excellent products that could definitely sell more if only they could crack the market, and distribution seems to be the key.

Unfortunately, making an acquisition in Japan is not easy, although, it has at least, been getting somewhat easier.[2] There are problems of two sorts, each of them familiar elsewhere but even more complicated in Japan than most liberal economies.

The first is related to the cherished concept of the company as a living entity, one to which not only the owner but the personnel are attached. This is further aggravated by the existence of lifetime employment in many firms, which, although not written into the contract, is regarded as morally binding. Japanese employees do not like being taken over by another management because they are not certain that the many unwritten rules will be heeded. And this is particularly important if the acquirers are foreigners who are widely viewed as not knowing the rules to begin with, not treating personnel with the same care, and often not being around for the long haul and thus little concerned by the ultimate fate of the company or its personnel.

To make an acquisition, it is indispensable to overcome this kind of fear, a process that can be very slow and time-consuming, as well as costly. It is necessary to reassure the managers and workers alike that their jobs will not be sacrificed and, if anything, an improvement can be expected. It helps to show commitment to the future by developing long-term plans and installing new machinery that shows a will to expand and upgrade. This will probably also involve raising wages and offering more vacation and perks than Japanese rivals.

Even then, the Japanese company being sought after may not trust the foreign acquirer or accept to deal with it directly. There is frequently a need of some intermediary, a go-between who can gently and diplomatically explain the advantages and bring the two sides closer together. This may be another company that does business with both, a respected businessman or senior official (usually retired), or a consultant or broker. Given the need for trust and familiarity, it often turns out that the smoothest acquisitions or mergers are arranged between companies that have already been working together, namely the foreign company and its existing distributors or joint venture partners.

The other kind of difficulty is basically financial. Obviously, there is the huge price Japanese companies command at present. But that is actually easier to solve than the fact that most are well protected from unwanted suitors by the existence of what is known as "stable cross-holding of shares." Companies that do business together, that depend on one another, that are part of a larger grouping or *keiretsu* traditionally hold shares in one another. Since cross-holdings can exist with the bank, suppliers, clients, and related companies, it may actually amount to a majority of the shares. These shares are not traded freely and are quite hard to come by.

While a hostile takeover is not impossible, it would not be easy for foreigners in particular, as Boone Picken's experience with Koito amply showed. Not only would it be hard to acquire enough shares, other friendly companies holding on to theirs, they might even buy more. And it would be impossible to run such a company given the negative reactions of the bank, suppliers, clients, and others who would find their own relationships with the company altered. To this must be added the lack of cooperation by the existing managers and workers.

The result is that most acquisitions are indeed friendly. And they are usually limited to Japanese companies that act under duress, because they are in difficult financial straits or due to failure of a major product. Consequently, they accept being taken over by a foreign company that can provide necessary financing, new products or new markets. This means that the acquirer is probably paying a considerable premium. Thus, any acquisitions must be carefully thought out in advance and fit into a long-term strategy for penetrating the Japanese market.

Practical Examples

Yet, despite the difficulty and cost, there have been more and more acquisitions and mergers over recent years. It is also known that many more are in the pipeline. Indeed, this has now become a very definite alternative whereas, in earlier years, it was a rarity and often shunned by foreigners because they did not know if they could successfully absorb or manage such firms. While it is still premature to seek clearcut trends, the results on the whole have been favorable, and many foreign companies have increased their presence, enhanced their image and expanded sales faster than would have otherwise been possible.

Among the notable acquisitions, many have been of local distributors, which were strongly desired to boost and also control marketing efforts. Examples are most prevalent in the pharmaceutical sector, with Rorer Group acquiring Kyoritsu and Toho, Merck, Banyu and Torii, and Merrell Dow, Funai. Corning Glass Works took over ALS and Asahi Medical, both medical equipment distributors. And Eastman Kodak bought three units of Kasuda Business Machines, an information equipment distributor.[3]

Naturally, takeovers in the pharmaceutical sector were not limited to distribution concerns, the firms also being producers in their own right. Other companies have sought production knowhow or captive facilities, with Data General acquiring Nippon Mini-Computer (computers and components); Motorola, Aizu-Toko (semiconductors); Emerson Electric, Ueshima Seisakusho (meters and testers); and Coopervision, Takeda (ophthalmic instruments).

In many cases, the two parties had been doing business for years already, so the transfer was greatly facilitated. This includes most of the pharmaceutical firms as well as the acquisitions of former subcontractors by manufacturers. In many instances, what actually happened was that the foreign joint venture partner bought out the Japanese party. This occurred for GE, Pfizer, Campbell Soup, and TRW.

There were clear advantages to this. The two parties knew one another better, they had greater trust, and they knew what the deal was worth. This obviated the need for a go-between and merely involved strengthening and adjusting older relations rather than creating new ones. More and more, however, brokers have been offering smaller companies for sale, much as happens in the West. And Yamaichi Securities smoothed the way for Corning's acquisition of Tokina's Nasco unit.[4]

Frequently, the process has been gradual, a sort of "creeping" merger or acquisition. This leaves both parties time to adjust and decide whether to go further. For example, when Bayer Yakuhin was first established in 1979, the equity breakdown was Bayer 50 percent, Takeda 30 percent, and Yoshitomi Pharmaceutical 20 percent. Only a decade later, it had shifted in Bayer's favor, with over 75 percent.[5] Similarly, Hewlett-Packard raised its share of the joint venture with Yokogawa Electric from 51 percent to 75 percent.[6] In the case of Corning Japan, it first had its two distributors merge and took only a one-third share. Later on, it bought its partners out.[7]

Notes

1. *Wall Street Journal*, August 9, 1990, p. C1.

2. See Abegglen and Stalk, op. cit., pp. 231-39.

3. "If You Can't Beat 'Em, Buy 'Em: Takeovers Arrive In Japan," *Business Week*, September 29, 1986, pp. 80-81.

4. Ibid., p. 81.

5. "How to Succeed in the Japanese Market," *Tokyo Business Today*, July 1990, pp. 27-31.

6. *The Oriental Economist*, June, 1985, p. 10.

7. *Business Week*, op. cit., p. 81.

VI

Mutual Adjustments

Doing Like the Japanese

Frequently one hears of complaints by foreign firms attempting to enter into the Japanese market that their products do poorly in Japan, in spite of selling well abroad and in third countries. Such situations highlight that working with the Japanese distribution system also requires that a firm achieve market fit with regard to societal demands. This chapter highlights the importance of such market fit, without which market success will remain elusive. It explains the major dimensions to which companies must adhere in order to become a part of the traditional Japanese cultural and social setting in the business world. The major guiding principle is that when in Japan, a firm must do as the Japanese do themselves and expect from others.

The Quality Imperative

Even though the Japanese obsession with quality has led to some ridicule in the popular press, the taunting is also accompanied by a healthy dose of worry. The quality of Japanese goods is extremely high, and has been a primary reason for Japan's success in its domestic market and the global economy. Lack of quality is the major, insurmountable barrier for foreign firms.

Quality considerations are simply first and foremost on the minds of many Japanese consumers and are catered to successfully by Japanese firms. While the 1960s and 70s witnessed a major emphasis on acquisition by consumers, increased wealth in the '80s and '90s has brought selectivity, the desire for a very high quality of life expressed through highly selective product purchases, and a lack of willingness for compromise. Perfection has come to be expected. For example, leather goods with even slight discolorations, which are fully acceptable elsewhere, are discarded by the Japanese. One U.S. maker of high-priced T-shirts had an entire shipment rejected because the seams had little stitching holes when the shirt was stretched. As the Japanese customer explained: "We expect high-quality items to include hidden effort, even in areas that don't show. Whether that's really necessary is a different matter." The same standards are also applied to industrial products, as the Bendix corporation found out when it supplied Toyota with disc brake pads. Matt Yoshida of Bendix Japan recalls that "in the U.S., the quality of a part is judged to be satisfactory if it functions properly. But in Japan, perfection is expected over portions that have nothing to do with function, such as the finish of the paint job."[1]

Knowing about the high standards of their customers, members of the distribution channel want to be certain that they can live up to expectations. As a result, they will carefully inspect merchandise at all levels and unhesitatingly return entire shipments if occasional defects are found. Channel members also want to be certain that a quality control system exists at the point of manufacture that is up to par with Japanese standards, so that problems will not arise in the first place. Consequently, the importer must be able to provide such assurances and live up to them. A good example of service expectations and responsiveness is provided by the reflections of a marketing manager of OSRAM Ltd., a subsidiary of the German Siemens AG, which supplies the Japanese market with headlight halogen lamps.

> In not only Germany, but all countries outside of Japan, the basic quality control stance is that among several hundreds of thousands of products, the appearance of a few flawed pieces is inevitable, so all that is necessary is replacement of such items. But in Japan, a single flawed piece is considered highly problematic. In the case of automobile makers, who are particularly strict about quality, demands are made for detailed reports on clarification of the cause and countermeasures to be taken for the appearance of even a single flawed piece, and if such reports are not forthcoming, they will discontinue further transactions. It was extremely difficult to convince the German home office to provide such "unprecedented" reports in the early days. We finally persuaded them that such reports were necessary to convince the users of our reliability. Once persuaded, however, they quickly set out with

a will to provide such reports and improve product quality. As a result, quality that met with the demands of the users was achieved in an extremely short time.[2]

What drives the point home even more is the fact that the same manager states, "Eventually, we hope to build a production base in Japan through which we can provide even more complete and high quality services." This statement shows that even excellent levels of quality are in need of continuous improvement.

The quality message has been received and to a large degree absorbed by U.S. firms and policy makers, as the example of the creation of and competition for the prestigious Malcolm Baldrige National Quality Award shows. Firms entering Japan, however, are well advised to continually remind themselves of the uncompromisability of quality, to start out by checking and comparing the quality levels expected and delivered by their Japanese competitors, and to be prepared to match or even exceed these standards.

The Importance of Price

Western observers often hear reports of the affluent Japanese, who are purchasing record amounts of expensive imports, including cars, jewelry, or art. Many have seen the Japanese tourists buying out the local Gucci and Hermes stores. As a result, an impression has been formed that Japanese consumers are oblivious to prices. While this may be true for some segments of the population such as the "new rich," the "bachelor aristocrats," or the *ol-kizoku* (office lady nobility), and for some products that connote status, face, or quality of life, price plays a major role for many consumers and products.

Surveys by the Japanese government indicate that many consumers are displaying significant discontent about the high prices of products.[3] To a large degree, these feelings of disgruntlement have grown due to a lack of impact of *endaka* (the high value of the yen) on the prices of imports. The yen appreciation and the fall in oil prices chipped in more than 29 trillion yen into the Japanese economy between October of 1985 and January of 1988. According to the Economic Planning Agency of Japan, no more than 11 trillion yen was actually passed through to consumers in the form of lower prices. The remaining 18 trillion yen appear to have been retained as extra profits by importers, distributors, and retailers.[4]

Pressured by high housing prices and increasing cost of living, Japanese consumers turn out to be quite similar to their American or European counterparts: they want a bargain and are increasingly willing to seek out retailers who offer inexpensive goods and services. Particularly the youth market, salarymen, and retirees, but also many middle-income earners, are looking for cheap buys on ordinary products that do not add to face and status. In a 1990 survey, 70 percent of respondents indicated that they favored reasonable prices over high-priced "quality" goods.[5]

In many instances, this price-consciousness drives purchasers towards imports from newly industrialized countries (NICs). Both consumers and producers are learning from experience that, contrary to their old belief, a cheaper price no longer connotes an inferior product. And even if some quality or service compromises have to be made, a steep discount can well compensate for these shortcomings.

Japanese intermediaries have responded to the challenge by drastically increasing their imports of products from NICs. In addition, new forms of distribution highlight the low price aspects. Discount outlets are rapidly increasing their market share. Unlike the glamorous Ginza department stores, where uniformed ladies in white gloves bow as one enters, the service at these outlets is more than basic by Japanese standards. There is usually no delivery, no wrapping, no insurance, no installment payment plan, no explanation of how to use the item and sometimes even no product on display. Young people crowd these shops which sell televisions, stereos and similar products for 10 to 20 percent below "normal" prices. There one can find a 19-inch Korean-made color TV for $43, marked down from $70. By comparison, a Sony in the Ginza costs up to $500.[6]

These discount practices are only one pressure on the traditional Japanese intermediaries. *Endaka* has made exporting more difficult. As a result, Japanese firms are concentrating more on their domestic market, thus intensifying competition among themselves. Increasingly, this competition has led to reverse imports from Japanese-owned plants abroad. For example, Hitachi in early 1988 began to reverse import small refrigerators and electrical fans from its plant in Thailand and 21-inch color televisions from its plant in Taiwan.[7] In addition, *endaka* has resulted in an increase of gray market imports, resulting in a flood of unauthorized, but genuine, products from abroad. For example, in Ikebukuro, a major shopping area in Tokyo, a large discount retailer sells Fuji film at a discount. However, the package carries the Korean language, not Japanese. It was meant to be sold in Korea, but made its way into the Japanese market.[8] Similarly, a discount store in Tokyo started selling Matsushita cordless telephones that it had re-imported from New York for a mere 40 percent of the Tokyo list price used in the manufacturer's own shops. Matsushita tried to buy back the entire consignment. Bargain-hunters got there first.[9]

The bottom line is the fact that price competition in Japan has heated up enormously over the past few years. Consumers have grown more price-conscious, and manufacturers and intermediaries are responding. The foreign firm, in spite of frequently cited historical evidence to the contrary, should realize that price has become a powerful motivator.

Product Holism

Both consumers and channel members have a tendency to hold a holistic view of products, which means that the total product, with all its tangible and intangible components, is considered. For example, the packaging of products is considered an integral part of the purchase. Even slight faults or stains on the wrapping make a product unsalable. But the view of holism goes further than packaging. From a manufacturing perspective, the goal is to provide the customers with more "value" in the products they purchase. Product value is determined by cost and quality factors. In the United States, management typically sees cost reduction and quality improvement as contradictory objectives, particularly when quality is perceived and mainly measured by choice of materials or engineering tolerances. By contrast, Japanese firms see cost reduction and quality improvements as parallel objectives that go in tandem. The Japanese word *keihakutansho* epitomizes the drive by Japanese firms to create value by simultaneously lowering cost and increasing quality. *Keihakutansho* literally means "lighter, slimmer, shorter, and smaller," and thus implies less expensive and more useful products that are economical in purchase, use and maintenance.[10]

Consumer and channel demand also focuses strongly on precision in product appropriateness. This means that products need to be truly superior and offer a precise match with needs in order to be successful. Also-ran products are likely to have a short life span.

In order to achieve this match, Japanese firms are willing to go to great lengths in their research and observation of customer needs. All this work often results in only subtle differences involving color, size, shape, taste, or product composition, but can spell major marketing success.[11] For example, Toyota recently sent a group of its engineers and designers to Southern California to nonchalantly "observe" how women get in and operate their cars. They found that women with long fingernails have trouble opening the door of their cars and operating various knobs on the dashboard. Naturally, Toyota engineers and designers were able to "understand" the women's plight and redraw some of their automobile exterior and interior designs.[12]

Foreign firms are expected to do the same, and many are doing so. For example, electric shavers were especially developed to fit the size of Japanese hands. Salomon S.A., a French manufacturer of ski equipment, recognized early on that the physical proportions of the Japanese are slightly different from Europeans. As a representative explained, "Japanese women, particularly from the knee down, can be a problem to fit. So we have to take this into account when designing our products. But the young generation is taller, and their proportions are rapidly approaching that of Europeans."[13] Spalding Japan's sales tripled from 200,000 to 600,000 units when the firm adapted American designs to the Japanese physique. With lower weights and thinner grips, Japanese golfers now find Spalding golf clubs a perfect fit.[14] Johnson & Johnson recognized the Japanese cultural sensitivity to colors and fragrances, and reformulated its Baby Lotion to be white and much less scented than its U.S. product. The product became a hit in Japan. A German firm, specializing in Angora wool products even developed an entirely new product, "Setany," which is made of silk and cotton, rather than Angora, in order to fit with the warm and humid climate conditions of Japan and the tastes for apparel products of the Japanese people.[15]

However, there are also many occasions where unwillingness or inability to adapt has caused sales relationships to falter. The unwillingness of U.S. manufacturers to adapt to market requirements has perhaps become most widely known internationally by the refusal to change the side of the steering wheel for cars exported to Japan. The same problem, however, also exists on the part of small manufacturers. Executives of one Japanese department store, for example, produced eight years of correspondence with U.S. furniture manufacturers. Apart from quality issues, these letters dealt mainly with the need for furniture to be downsized in order to match up with Japanese market needs. Given the smaller bodies of the Japanese and smaller living spaces, only smaller furniture would provide a good "fit" for the Japanese customer. However, despite substantial prodding and advice, this department store was not able to locate a single U.S. furniture manufacturer willing to reduce the size of standard furniture. As a result, the store decided to purchase British goods from a manufacturer more willing to make such changes. In light of the fact that furniture imports into Japan have grown from $347 million in 1986 to $815 million in 1988,[16] such loss of business to U.S. firms is regrettable.

Clearly, the decision to make such adaptive changes is not an easy one. When considering the economies of scale of production and the often initially limited size of the market, cost calculations may indicate that such adjustments are prohibitively expensive. However, overall market potential in the long run, not just in Japan, but also in other nations where customers may have similar needs and preferences, may make such cost a necessary investment.

Reliability and Service

As mentioned previously, but well-deserving of reiteration, product quality considerations are paramount in the Japanese market. In spite of the already existing high standards, however, material and human fallibility still results in the occasional product breakdown. In these instances, Japanese customers and channel members expect major service back-up, no matter what the cost, with virtually no time delay. Service or *sa-bi-su* is a highly regarded component of a product and expected throughout the lifetime of a business relationship. Spirax Sarco Ltd., a British manufacturer of steam valves, for example, provides a correspondence course principally for people who must put together the piping for steam systems.

The firm will also send textbooks on systems, which have been translated to Japanese, free to any customers who ask for one.

Simply stressing product performance over maintenance can turn out to be a grave oversight,[17] since, in the selection of merchandise, buyers show a major interest in whether or not careful and speedy service is offered. Major expense in performing such service on part of importers, while perhaps admirable from a non-Japanese perspective, will be acknowledged but only as "doing what is right and expected" on the Japanese side.

On-Time Delivery

Given existing space constraints, excellent delivery performance is a must. While the importance of delivery times has been emphasized and accepted in the production environment and led to the JIT (just-in-time) manufacturing concept, Japanese channel members and customers expect it also at their level. In many instances, for example, department stores will deliver a customer's purchases immediately to the home. Waiting periods of several months for new merchandise or even a temporary out-of-stock situation are seen as very detrimental to a business relationship. Efforts to meet market needs in spite of adversity are hailed and appreciated. For example, Anheuser-Busch, in collaboration with Suntory, a Japanese whiskey and beer producer, decided several years ago to take a promotional campaign to Japan for the annual June gift-giving season. The promotion was such a success that a stock-out occurred, leaving Suntory in the embarrassing position of not being able to fill its orders. Anheuser-Busch filled a Boeing 747 freighter aircraft with cases of Budweiser and flew them to Japan. Although the company spent roughly $1 million to bring the beer to Japan, it won millions more in free publicity and, more importantly, earned an enormous reservoir of good will with Suntory.[18]

The Long-Term Perspective

Working with Japanese firms and customers is done not on a transaction basis, but rather on a relationship basis. When dealing with a foreign firm or product on the Japanese side, it is only rarely the transaction at hand that governs the day. Rather, emphasis rests with long-term cooperation and collaboration, cultural fit, and the question of "where will we be five years from now?" Clearly, U.S. firms have to deal with substantial real and perceived shortcomings in this area. The frequently held Japanese view of U.S. firms is summarized perhaps best in the controversial book by Morita and Ishihara, where Morita deplores "The decline of an America that can only see ten minutes ahead."[19] He compares the 10-minute perspective of the United States with a 10-year perspective of Japan.

As discussed in previous chapters, the entire Japanese economic and business relationship system is oriented towards the long term. Leases have to be signed for 10 years, customers are only gradually developed, market penetration and market share rather than short-term returns are emphasized. The existing doubt about U.S. firms acts as a severe shortcoming in penetrating Japan, ranging from potential customer doubts about ongoing product service, to channel misgivings about continued product development and support, to the difficulty in attracting highly qualified personnel due to their desire for long-term employment. U.S. firms, and for that matter, any foreign firm, therefore, need to determine from the outset of their planning to enter Japan to what degree management is committed to the venture and willing to stick with it. Once that internal commitment is generated, it needs to be clearly and fully communicated to the Japanese market, since it will shape the foundation of the business relationship.

Notes

1. *Jetro Monitor,* 1 September 1987.

2. *Focus Japan,* May 1988, p. 8.

3. "Distribution System Facing Big Changes," *Focus Japan,* March 1990.

4. Nicholas Valery, "Crunch in the Ginza-dori," *BZW Pacific,* February 1989, p. 11.

5. Shigeru Hoshino, "For Quality-Conscious Japanese Consumers, Low Prices Also Matter," *Tokyo Business Today,* September 1990, pp. 50–52.

6. See "Structural Changes in Japan's Distribution System," *JEI Report,* November 10, 1989; and Carla Rapoport, "Ready, Set, Sell—Japan Is Buying," *Fortune,* September 11, 1989.

7. William L. Brooks, "Japan's Distribution System in Flux," delivered at the 37th Japan-Western United States Association Professional Committee Meeting, Hakone, Japan, January 20, 1989.

8. Robert E. Weigand, "The Gray Market Comes to Japan," *Columbia Journal of World Business,* Fall 1989, p. 18.

9. "The Opening of Japan," *The Economist,* December 17, 1988, p. 70.

10. Michael R. Czinkota and Masaaki Kotabe, "Product Development the Japanese Way," *Journal of Business Strategy,* November/December 1990, pp. 31–36.

11. John T. Enright, "Selling Consumer Goods in Japan," *Business America* (Washington, D.C.: U.S. Department of Commerce, March 3, 1986), pp. 2–5.

12. Czinkota and Kotabe, op. cit.

13. "Downhill Skiers Mean Rising Sales," *Focus Japan*, February 1989, p. 8.
14. *Focus Japan*, March 1990, p. 8.
15. *Focus Japan*, February 1988, p. 8.
16. "Wooden Furnishings Gaining Popularity in Japan," *Jetro Monitor* 5, 2, May 1990, pp. 1–2.
17. "This American Firm Isn't Complaining About Japan," *Marketing News*, July 9, 1990, p. 21.
18. Keith N. Rockwell, "Playing by Japan's Rules Pays Off," *The Journal of Commerce*, December 29, 1989, p. 5A.
19. Akio Morita and Shinichiro Ishihara, *The Japan that Can Say "No"* (Tokyo: Kobunsha, 1989).

C H A P T E R

Coming Closer Together

The Japanese market differs in many respects from Western economies. However, the business system is undergoing substantial change as a reflection of changes in society. Business institutions are faced with major shifts in demand and a gradually increasing unwillingness on the part of consumers to pay unnecessarily high prices and be deprived of the rightful fruits of their labors.

These developments bode well for foreign businesses waiting to break into the Japanese market. Change is, after all, the key opportunity for the marketer. However, it must be understood that most of the market shifts taking place now neither result from, nor are they amenable to, substantial government intervention. Rather they are the outcome of societal change to which the government has been responsive. Such societal change is always likely to be gradual and may result in institutional configurations in which process outpaces structure. In such instances, the marketer must focus on the underlying dynamics of the system rather than on the encrusted formations on its surface.

Thus, it is important to recognize the human element of the Japanese business system and the social repercussions of change. The system will not adjust on the basis of business economics alone, but rather on the basis of societal economics.

Despite some need to allow the changes in the Japanese market to occur at their own pace, there are steps that the Japanese and foreign public and private sectors need to undertake to enhance global economic relations. To aid in this process, several programmatic steps are outlined here

The Japanese Private Sector

The private sector in Japan must finally come to recognize that Japan is facing an import imperative. Much of its prosperity has depended on an international market that is relatively free of constraints, particularly in the case of the United States. However, as trade imbalances between Japan and its major trading partners continue, Japanese access to foreign markets becomes threatened. If Japanese firms expect to retain their international market access, they must demonstrate a willingness to reciprocate the benefits that have allowed them this access.

Changes in attitude should include a serious consideration of the international trade repercussions of any heretofore domestic business decision. For example, it will be of increasing importance to consider sourcing outside one's *keiretsu* or looking beyond established channel members and give recognition to supply alternatives from abroad. Japanese firms must now consider the necessity of forging new ties and relationships with foreign firms. They have already recognized that economy of scale considerations, combined with the rising cost of research and development, make it mandatory to enter markets on a global scale. These requirements apply to foreign firms as well. Therefore, Japanese firms, in a very self-serving manner, will need to participate in further market openings in order to preserve their own future. Years of intense domestic competition have prepared Japanese firms well for such new entrants. After all, this heated competition is, to a large degree, responsible for the global preeminence of Japanese producers. Competitors from abroad will therefore serve to strengthen, rather than weaken, the Japanese economy.

Firms Outside Japan

Non-Japanese firms desiring to do more business in Japan also must undergo some transformation. First and foremost, businesses must recognize that they cannot afford not to be in the Japanese market. For one, it would seem unwise not to tap a market of 120 million consumers with large amounts of disposable income. More important, however, is the fact that by not confronting the competition head-on, a firm runs the danger of missing out on honing competitive skills that it will be in dire need of once Japanese firms enter its own home market. Like it or not, the business world has become globalized, and the Japanese market has become a key node. Third, firms need to understand the constraints of the Japanese market and develop a willingness and ability to work within those constraints. Such understanding will require adjustments in corporate thinking about international operation in order to penetrate the Japanese market successfully.

Many international business executives still hold a very dim view of the openness of Japanese markets, a view frequently shaped by experiences of the past and sometimes based on the realities of the present. However, with positive developments in the Japanese market now occurring, it is up to the business community to take advantage of these new opportunities.

For example, the new chain stores emerging in Japan can become valuable allies to importers since they may be willing to change the composition of their merchandise offering. In addition, a centralized purchasing function can provide for large-sized orders that would otherwise be difficult to obtain. The centralized distribution employed by many of these chain stores enables their local headquarters to provide many service functions that would be difficult for a foreign supplier to deliver.

In a similar vein, exporters should cooperate more fully with Japanese cash-and-carry wholesalers and discount retailers. Because of their frequent lack of allegiance to any specific manufacturer and their primary focus on price and product, these firms have the potential to become good partners. While the type of clientele attracted by these stores may restrict the line of merchandise that can be offered, their continued growth will open up more opportunities. Their main focus will remain on price and product competitiveness, factors on which foreign firms will need to concentrate.

Similar opportunities for exports also exist with other emerging channel participants. For example, the increase in non-store retailing has opened up new opportunities in the mail order sector. The willingness of Japanese consumers to accept this direct method of distribution, circumventing existing institutional barriers, may be the greatest single asset of this innovative form of market penetration. Also, the trend toward order consolidation and the establishment of new transportation companies offers new avenues for cooperation. Most of the new transportation firms are not tied to any specific channel member, but rather aim at providing the most efficient service. In doing so, they are an important complementary ingredient for competitive distribution in Japan.

Foreign firms should also take advantage of the Japanese information revolution. It is now easier to conduct market research with good, quick results that permit a more targeted market segmentation approach. The improved information flow has also reduced the need for inventory size and, therefore, the level of necessary initial investment.

In order for a foreign firm to benefit from any of these changes, it must improve its own international competitiveness. Firms should increase their focus on product quality, product consistency, price, and high service delivery. Furthermore, doing business in Japan does not necessarily imply a departure from all known business rules. Many features of the Japanese business system described in this book are also an integral part of most domestic business environments. For example, managers outside of Japan have formal and informal ties among themselves as well (be it at a club or at the golf course). Non-Japanese channel members also expect service, financing, promotional assistance, and return privileges. It is in the performance and intensity of these activities, however, where the difference from the Japanese market emerges. Japanese business practices may ⩗ require heavier time, financial and quality commitments than elsewhere.

Not every firm will be able to afford the long-term commitment of managerial time and financial resources necessary to compete successfully in Japan. For example, even though a firm may know that success for its products mandates the maintenance of a warehouse, the stationing of service technicians, and the establishment of a local presence in Japan, this is not always feasible given limited resources. The decision often boils down to whether there will be enough product sales or sufficient profits generated to justify the expenditures. Currently, in analyzing cost versus profit potential, many firms decide to forgo opportunities.

In some instances, this decision may be correct. In many cases, however, the time element used may be deficient. Without a doubt, successful market performance in Japan does require substantial commitments. The key one among these is that of time. As a result, start-up operations may be lengthier and more expensive than elsewhere. However, the long-term benefits may also be greater. Foreign firms should, therefore, lengthen the time horizon used for business decisions when dealing with Japan, and, in light of Japan's past economic performance, reduce the discount factor when determining the net present value of their actions.

Exporting firms should also consider a consortium approach. Firms that are unable to make major commitments based on their own resources may consider joining forces with other companies. Market entry would be much easier if a firm had to support only 10 percent of the cost of a warehouse or of a service technician. It is here that, for U.S. firms, the mechanism of the export trading company (ETC) can prove to be a major supporting factor for successful business development abroad. Even though this mechanism has not been used much to date, it offers major potential for export cooperation among firms.

Foreign firms should also seriously consider a reorientation from exporting to direct investment. Many facets of the Japanese market indicate that there is no substitute for close market contact. Nothing will demonstrate a firm's commitment to success more clearly than the establishment of an operation in the country. Even though such a decision brings with it a host of obstacles, investment is becoming less difficult as formerly restrictive Japanese employment practices and investment obstacles are easing.

Japan's Policy

The upper echelons of the Japanese policy community have recognized the need to increase Japan's imports. This has led to the implementation of unique trade policies. After all, few nations have public and private bodies allocating funds to help increase the exports of their trading partners. However, any package of import expansion measures also requires a move away from the traditional bureaucratic perspective of defense against imports. These bureaucratic attitudes often have been shaped for decades by the grim necessity for exports. In some cases, change can be brought about only by the gradual extinction of old bureaucratic warhorses.

In shaping new trade relations, Japan's public sector must address both reality and perception. A change in the reality of the Japanese marketplace requires the understanding that there are indeed obstacles to the importation of foreign products and to foreign direct investment, and that a reduction of these obstacles is necessary and beneficial to Japan. There may not be that much the Japanese government can do about the existence of close commercial relations between private corporations, either as *keiretsu* or looser groupings. Yet, to the extent that these result in more closed markets, the government must do what little it can. It can at least ensure that these relations do not exceed the bounds set by national antitrust legislation and reinforce the Fair Trade Commission so that it becomes a more effective watchdog. Indeed, since some of these relations may hurt domestic consumers, it might consider the possibility of stricter rules in the national interest as well as in the interest of international harmony. Moreover, since its market system is more constricted by such commercial arrangements than that of many of its trading partners, Japan should take further measures to facilitate entry along the lines of the trade fairs and assistance provided by MIPRO, JETRO, and other bodies. At the very least, it should act swiftly to eliminate remaining tariffs, quotas, non-tariff barriers, and administrative impediments, since foreign companies will have to contend with the commercial barriers anyway.

Perceptions of the Japanese market are the second item the public sector must address. Often these perceptions matter just as much as, and sometimes more than, reality. Since negative beliefs about trading partners increase during periods of economic difficulties and large trade imbalances, it is vital that Japan address this issue rapidly. In particular, changes within the Japanese market will be insufficient if they are not communicated properly. A trickle-down approach to the dissemination of information may be too slow. As a result of preconceived notions, Japanese trade relations may become aggravated to such an extent that actual changes will matter very little.

For U.S. institutions and individuals, for example, the issue of fairness is very important. As a recent opinion poll notes, already over two-thirds of the American people regard Japan as more threatening than the Soviet Union. And about 60 percent of American consumers have expressed a willingness to boycott Japanese goods if Japan does not abandon its "unfair" trade practices.[1] In a democratic society, such popular feelings are likely to eventually be translated into policy actions. A perception of fairness is not achieved by steps such as the use of industry associations for certification or regulatory purposes. While this practice may be quite acceptable in Japan, and even though this process may run more smoothly if it is regulated by Japanese citizens only, rather than by both Japanese and foreign citizens, it does create the impression of unfairness. Such impressions, regardless of their factual merits, will continue to hurt trading relations and must, therefore, be addressed. Similarly, announcements of market-opening efforts that do not describe at the same time the expected results, together with clear time delineations, will be ridiculed and dismissed as simple public relations tactics. In addition to the import imperative to be addressed by the private sector in Japan, the public sector must facilitate these imports and concurrently make major efforts to achieve international trade transparency.

Even though many restrictive measures exist mainly for domestic Japanese policy reasons rather than to restrict the importation of foreign products, their international repercussions are severe. For example, pressure blocs emanating from the farm sector shape domestic policymaking. However, the effects of such domestic policy on foreign trading partners must be considered with greater sensitivity, especially given increasing protectionistic pressures worldwide. It is insufficient to attempt to deflect foreign market access demands by pointing to domestic policy concerns. Japan has become economically too predominant and interdependent to continue to largely ignore foreign economic demands or interests.

In order to maintain its own long-term economic health, Japan must now fully integrate the legitimate concerns of its trading partners into its domestic policy planning. Such integration does not refer to periodic packages developed to assuage foreign concerns. Nor does it indicate that marginal increases in foreign exports to Japan are the key. Rather, it points towards a policy that is predicated on Japan's accomplished role as a major economic power, and accepting of the responsibilities that accompany such an achievement, even if acting on these responsibilities causes domestic pain. **There can be no leadership without sacrifices.** Just as Japanese authorities continuously remind the U.S. of the need for a long-term perspective, they themselves need to recognize the validity of this concept to their own policy-making as well. As history has shown us, the long-term future of an isolated Japan looks dim.

Just as the risks and costs of new product developments have become too high for individual firms to absorb, some of the risks and costs facing governments and this world have become too large for any one country to handle. These issues go far beyond the comparatively mundane concerns about trade and investment. They refer to global responsibilities that will shape the next century for humankind.

The needs of the newly-democratized countries of Eastern Europe, of the debtor nations and of the developing world are only one set of issues. They are accompanied by global concerns, such as preoccupation with the pollution of air and water, global warming and the maintenance of our entire ecosystem. They are further augmented by the breakout of new diseases, major regional conflicts, such as the one in the Middle East, and sudden shifts in the world's energy supply situation. All of these issues point towards an increased fragility of the world we live in.

Japan must accept the major responsibility resting upon the country to participate, if not in the solution, at least in the control or amelioration of these issues. As a result, Japanese policy must integrate itself into the world, offering co-leadership and a major commitment of the Japanese nation. Japan can no longer afford to narrowly look only for its own immediate benefit, but must instead share its accomplishments, achievements, and markets with the world. In the long term, this apparently altruistic view will ensure Japan's survival.

Policies By Trading Partners

Foreign policymakers also have responsibilities to improve trade relations. With Japan, they must develop a coherent and cohesive global trade strategy. United States trade officials, for example, cannot continue to trip over each other's luggage at Narita airport. The responsibility for trade policy must be unified and accorded the same national priority as any other trillion dollar economic activity. At the same time, trade policy must be placed in its relevant context within global issues in general.

The United States must temper its desire for equal market access **but rather demand and accept equivalent concessions** across the board. Determining such equivalence, particularly for the longer run, requires detailed information. Once the bargaining chips have been determined, however, equivalence must be placed in the context of a time frame and revised periodically so that the outcome results in a resolution rather than a delay of trade disputes.

United States policymakers—Congress, the president and his staff—need to be realistic about their time frames. Even though deadlines must be set in order to measure results, trade imbalances cannot be legislated away within a matter of days or weeks. Given the relatively short time between elections and the mere 15 months during which the average political appointee in the United States holds office, the desire to achieve major results within that time span is understandable. However, just as Japan's evolution from minor international player to trade superpower has not occurred overnight, the U.S. trade deficit is not the result of short-term factors.

To overcome problems such as declines in the growth rate of productivity, the adversarial relationship between government and business and between business and labor, the lack of international orientation on the part of U.S. firms, and the problems with the educational system, Japan-focused stop-gap solutions are insufficient. Such solutions would only result in a temporary "trade-managed" adjustment rather than successful market penetration abroad by U.S. firms. The reality is that U.S. policy-makers need to work hard on getting their own house in order. Low national savings rates have a major effect on investment into research, development, and human capital. Yet, public oratory stressing the need to save more is incomplete unless accompanied by the concommitant demand to spend less. A long history of overspending, on the part of individuals as well as government, has undermined the soundness of the economic foundation of the United States. In order to regain economic competitiveness and to live up to the leadership expectations placed on the United States by the world, the primary policy objective will have to be the restructuring of the domestic economy. In part, such restructuring will mean that the United States needs to become more Japanese in its consumption behavior, at the same time as policy discussions admonish Japan to become more American. Since voluntarism in terms of savings is a rare commodity, the most viable policy step will have to include the refurbishment of tax policies that reward saving and provide a disincentive to overspending. Such a step will be much more important than the attempt to locate receptive trading partners and financiers abroad. Even though it is most tempting to lay blame at the doorsteps of others, preferably nonvoters, the United States owes it to itself and to an interdependent world to take the first step in restoring its economic soundness.

On both sides of the Pacific, there is a need to eliminate the scapegoat mentality. The relationship, not only between Japan and the United States, but among all the countries globally tied to each other via the benefits of international trade, is far too important to become a sacrificial lamb on the altar of protectionism. We need to work together as partners, acknowledging and respecting our cultural and societal differences and striving for global improvement. This is a decade of collaboration and cooperation among the major trading nations, not confrontation. We need to begin talking with, not at, each other in order to promote change that is acceptable, tolerable, and beneficial for all participants. Trading nations no longer have regional or national markets and are no longer confronted with merely domestic concerns. National economic and domestic policies are clearly only fractional components of our global framework and will have to be subjugated to broader international considerations. This recognition must come about multilaterally, without scorn or ire, as an adaptation to new realities. Only then will it be possible to achieve our longing for a higher standard of living and a better quality of life.

Notes

1. *World Policy Institute Survey,* June 1989; and "Business Week/Harris Poll," *Business Week,* August 7, 1989, p. 51.

Glossary

depato	department store
endaka	yen appreciation
gaiatsu	foreign pressure
hakuraihin	Western imports, "luxuries"
kaisha	corporation
keihakutansho	lighter, thinner, shorter, smaller
keiretsu	corporate groupings or "alignments"
kigyo keiretsu	enterprise *keiretsu,* vertical grouping
kin'yu keiretsu	banking *keiretsu,* horizontal grouping
OL-kizoku	Office Lady or O.L. aristocracy
ryutsu keiretsu	distribution *keiretsu*
sa-bi-su	service
senmon shosha	small trading company
sogo shosha	general trading company
supa	supermarket

Acronyms

ACCJ	American Chamber of Commerce in Japan
ACTPN	Advisory Committee for Trade Policy and Negotiations
DKB	Dai-Ichi Kangyo Bank
FTC	Fair Trade Commission
GATT	General Agreement on Tariffs and Trade
IBJ	Industrial Bank of Japan
IHI	Ishikawajima-Harima Heavy Industries
JIT	Just In Time
JNR	Japanese National Railways
JETRO	Japan External Trade Organization
Keidanren	Japan Federation of Economic Organizations
LDP	Liberal Democratic Party
MIPRO	Manufactured Import Promotion Organization
MITI	Ministry of International Trade and Industry
NTB	Nontariff Barrier

NTT	Nippon Telegraph and Telephone
OECD	Organization for Economic Cooperation and Development
SII	Structural Impediments Initiative
USITC	United States International Trade Commission

Bibliography

Books

Abegglen, James C., *The Strategy of Japanese Business*. Cambridge: Ballinger, 1984.

_____ and George Stalk, Jr. *Kaisha, the Japanese Corporation*. New York: Basic Books, 1985.

Batzer, Erich, and Helmut Laumer, *Marketing Strategies and Distribution Channels for Foreign Companies in Japan*. Boulder: Westview Press, 1989.

CED, Strategy for U.S. Industrial Competitiveness. New York: Committee for Economic Development, 1984.

Christopher, Robert C., *Second to None: American Companies in Japan*. New York: Crown, 1987.

Czinkota, Michael R., and George Tesar, ed. *Export Management*. New York: Praeger, 1982.

Czinkota, Michael R., and Ilkka Ronkainen, *International Marketing* 2nd ed. Hinsdale, Ill.: Dryden Press, 1990.

DeMente, Boyd, *How to do Business with the Japanese*. Lincolnwood: NTC Publishing, 1987.

Destler, I.M. and Hideo Sato, eds., *Coping with U.S.-Japanese Economic Conflicts*. Lexington, Mass.: D.C. Heath, 1982.

Distribution Systems in Japan. An Original Study. Tokyo: Business Intercommunications, Inc, 1979.

Dodwell Marketing Consultants. *Direct Marketing in Japan*. Tokyo, 1990.

_____. *Industrial Goods Distribution in Japan*. Tokyo, 1987.

_____. *Industrial Groupings in Japan*. Tokyo, 1988.

_____. *Key Players in the Japanese Electronics Industry*. Tokyo, 1985.

_____. *Retail Distribution in Japan*. Tokyo, 1985.

_____. *The Structure of the Japanese Auto Parts Industry*. Tokyo, 1983.

_____. *The Structure of the Japanese Retail and Distribution Industry*. Tokyo, 1985.

Higashi, Chikara, *Japanese Trade Policy Formulation*. New York: Praeger, 1983.

HI-OVIS Project. Final Report, Phase I Experiment. Tokyo: Visual Information System Development Association, 1983.

Holloway, Robert J. and Akira Nagashima, *Multinationals in Japan*. Minneapolis: University of Minnesota, 1980.

Huddleston, Jackson N., Jr. *Gaijin Kaisha, Running a Foreign Business in Japan*. Armonk: M.E. Sharpe, 1990.

Hufbauer, Gary, Michael R. Czinkota, and Charles Trozzo, eds., *U.S. International Economic Policy, 1981*. Washington, D.C.: The International Law Institute, 1982.

Lincoln, Edward J., *Japan's Unequal Trade*. Washington, D.C.: Brookings Institution, 1990.

Morita, Akio, and Shinichiro Ishihara, *The Japan That Can Say "No" : The New U.S.-Japan Relations Card*. Tokyo: Kobunsha, 1989.

Nakane, Chie, *Japanese Society*. New York: Penguin Books, 1981.

Nevins, Thomas J., *Labor Pains and the Gaijin Boss—Hiring, Managing and Firing the Japanese*. Tokyo: Japan Times, 1984.

Pratt, Edward Ewing, *The Foreign Trade Handbook*. Chicago: The Dartnell Corporation, 1948.

Prestowitz, Clyde V., Jr., *Trading Places*. New York: Basic Books, 1988.

Richardson, Bradley M., and Taizo Ueda, eds., *Business and Society in Japan, Fundamentals for Businessmen.* East Asian Studies Program, Ohio State University. New York: Praeger, 1981.

Tokyo Keizai, *Japan Company Handbook.* Tokyo. Semiannual.

Tung, Rosalie L., *Business Negotiations With the Japanese.* Lexington: Lexington Books. 1984.

Van Wolferen, Karel, *The Enigma of Japanese Power.* New York: Vintage Books, 1989.

Woronoff, Jon, *Inside Japan, Inc.* Tokyo: Lotus Press, 1982.

_____. *Politics, the Japanese Way.* New York: St. Martin's and London: Macmillan, 1988.

_____. *World Trade War.* New York: Praeger, 1984.

Yamamura, Kozo, ed., *Policy and Trade Issues of the Japanese Economy.* Seattle: University of Washington Press, 1982.

Yoshihara, Kunio, *Sogo Shosha.* Tokyo: Oxford University Press, 1982.

Young, Alexander K., *The Sogo Shosha: Japan's Multinational Trading Companies.* Boulder: Westview Press, 1979.

Zimmerman, Mark, *How to do Business with the Japanese.* New York: Random House, 1985.

Reports and Articles

Ahern, Raymond J., "Market Access in Japan: The U.S. Experience." *Report #85-37E,* Washington, D.C.: Congressional Research Service, February 14, 1985.

Amagai, Jiro, "Japan's Distribution Industry: Short- and Long-term Prospects." *Business Japan,* July 1987.

American Chamber of Commerce in Japan. "Report on Trade Barriers, Membership Survey." Tokyo, 1982.

"Analysis of the U.S.–Japan Trade Problem." Report of the Advisory Committee for Trade Policy and Negotiations. February 1989.

Aoki, Hiromichi, "White Paper on International Trade 1989—Rapid Progress in Structural Adjustment." *Journal of Japanese Trade and Industry,* Vol. 8, No. 5, 1989.

"The Art of Distribution in Japan." *Traffic Management,* December 1989.

Asano, Ryosuke, "Networks Raise Efficiency of Distribution Information Systems." *Business Japan,* October 1989.

Bender, Paul S., "Breaking into Japan's Distribution System." *Traffic Management,* April 1988.

Berkwitt, George, "Japan's Three-Tiered Distribution." *Industrial Distribution,* July 1986.

Brock, William E., *Japanese Barriers to U.S. Trade and Recent Japanese Government Trade Initiatives.* Washington, D.C.: Office of the United States Trade Representative, November 1982.

_____. "William E. Brock on International Trade." *The Brookings Review,* Spring 1984.

Brooks, William L., "Japan's Distribution System in Flux." Delivered to the 30th Japan-Western United States Association Professional Committee Meeting, Makone, Japan, January 20, 1989.

Burton, Jack, and Dennis Chase, "Sun Still Not Shining on P&G in Japan." *Advertising Age,* December 20, 1982.

Businger, Donald, "Exports to Japan May Recover but Record U.S. Deficit is Likely." *Business America,* February 21, 1983.

"Cheaper Shopping in Japan." *The Economist,* January 28, 1989.

Clark, Lindley H. Jr., "Japan Must Do More for Its Consumers." *The Wall Street Journal,* December 8, 1989.

Covey, Amanda, "Vertical Restraints Under Japanese Law." *Law in Japan,* Vol. 14, 1981.

"Cracking the Japanese Market." Mainichi Daily News/Mainichi Newspapers. Tokyo, 1985.

Cullison, A.E., "Japan to Ease Distribution Rules to Boost Imports." *The Journal of Commerce,* September 18, 1989.

_____. "Japan to Ease Tough Controls on Retailers—Action Follows US Protest." *The Journal of Commerce,* February 27, 1990.

_____. "SII May Not Bury Barriers." *Journal of Commerce Special Report,* June 21, 1990.

Czinkota, Michael R., "Distribution of Consumer Products in Japan." *International Marketing Review,* Fall 1985.

_____. "Distribution in Japan: Problems and Changes." *Columbia Journal of World Business,* Fall 1985.

_____ and Masaaki Kotabe, "Product Development the Japanese Way." *The Journal of Business Strategy,* November/December 1990.

Deter, A. Robert, "Mail Order Marketing Starts Delivering Results." *Tradepia International,* No. 41, 1990.

Encarnation, Dennis J., and Mark Mason, "Neither MITI nor America: The Political Economy of Capital Liberalization in Japan." *International Organization,* 44, 1, Winter 1990.

Enright, Joseph T., "Selling Consumer Goods in Japan." *Business America,* March 3, 1986.

"Export-Import Bank Financing for Small Business." Hearing before the Subcommittee on Export Promotion and Market Development of the Committee on Small Business, United States Senate, Ninety-Eighth Congress, 1st Session, April 7, 1983.

"Export Promotion and Small Business." Hearing before the Subcommittee on Export Opportunities and Special Small Business Problems of the Committee on Small Business, House of Representatives, Ninety-Seventh Congress, September 21, 1982.

Fair Trade Commission, "The Fair Trade Commission's Approach to Trade Friction," April 1983.

Fields, George, "The Japanese Distribution System: Myths and Realities." *Tokyo Business Today,* July 1989.

Fukukawa, Shinji, "Cooperation and Free Trade." *Journal of Japanese Trade and Industry,* No. 2, 1989.

Haley, John O., "Marketing and Antitrust in Japan." *Hastings International and Comparative Law Review,* Vol. 2, No. 1, 1979.

"Helping High-Tech Firms into the Japanese Market." *Business America,* July 25, 1983.

Hirotaka, Takeuchi, and Louis P. Bucklin, "Productivity in Retailing: Retail Structure and Public Policy." *Journal of Retailing,* Vol. 53, No. 1, 1977.

_____. "In the Convenience Store Sector, Strategic Management Is a Must." *Japan Times,* December 1983.

Inako, T., "Culture in Business." *Journal of the ACCJ,* February 1983.

Ishida, Hideto, "Anticompetitive Practices in the Distribution of Goods and Services in Japan: The Problems of Distribution Keiretsu." *Journal of Japanese Studies,* Vol. 9, No. 2, Summer 1983.

"It's So Cheap." *The Economist,* May 14, 1988.

"Japan and Korea," *Business America,* October 31, 1983.

"Japan Business, Obstacles, and Opportunities." Prepared by McKinsey and Company, Inc., for the United States—Japan Trade Study Group, 1983.

The Japan Chamber of Commerce and Industry. "Distribution System and Market Access in Japan." Tokyo, June 1989.

The Japan Chamber of Commerce and Industry. "For Promoting Better Mutual Understanding." Undated.

Japan Economic Institute. "Japan's Distribution System: The Next Major Trade Confrontation?" No. 11a, Washington, D.C.: March 17, 1989.

_____. "Structural Changes in Japan's Distribution System." No. 43A, Washington, D.C. November 10, 1989.

"Japan Opens Its High-Tech Door a Little Wider." *Business Week,* February 6, 1984.

"Japan Outlines Major Program to Spur Imports." *The Journal Of Commerce,* January 2, 1990.

"Japan to Review Laws on Retail Stores." *The Journal of Commerce,* March 9, 1990.

"Japanese Consumers Still Waiting for Import Price Relief." *Business Asia,* November 9, 1987.

"Japanese Technology." Research Development Corporation of Japan (JRDC).

Johansson, Johny K., and Nonaka Ikujiro, "Japanese Exporting Marketing: Structures, Strategies, Counterstrategies." *International Marketing Review,* Vol. 1, No. 2, Winter 1983.

_____. "Special Report: Market Research the Japanese Way." *Harvard Business Review,* May–June 1987.

Johnson, Chalmers, "The 'Internationalization' of the Japanese Economy." *California Management Review,* Vol. 25, No. 3, Spring 1983.

"Jumping the Gun." *The Economist,* April 21, 1990.

Kawako, Hirofumi, "Japan and U.S. Tackle Structural Reform." *Journal of Japanese Trade and Industry,* Vol. 8, No. 6, 1989.

Kearney International, "Non-Tariff Barriers Affecting the Health Care Industry in Japan." Tokyo, 1980.

"Keizai Koho Center, Japan 1983." Japan Institute for Social and Economic Affairs. Tokyo, 1983.

Konaga, Keiichi, "Future of Japan's Distribution Industry." *Dentsu Japan Marketing/Advertising.* Spring Issue.

Lazer, William, Murata Shoji, and Kosaka Hiroshi, "Japanese Marketing: Towards a Better Understanding." *Journal of Marketing,* Vol. 49, No. 2, 1985.

Lehner, Urban C., and Alan Murray, "Strained Alliance: Will the U.S. Find the Resolve to Meet Japanese Challenge?" *The Wall Street Journal,* July 2, 1990.

McDermid, John F. "U.S.–Japan Trade: Problems and Prospects." *Fletcher Forum,* Vol. 7, No. 2, Summer 1983.

Mikami, Cindy, and Edward C. Baig, "Ready, Set, Sell—Japan Is Buying." *Fortune,* September 11, 1989.

Nagasaki, Takashi, "Discount Drinking." *Journal of Japanese Trade and Industry,* Vol. 8, No. 6, 1989.

Nagashima, Akira, "A Comparative 'Made-In' Product Image Survey Among Japanese Businessmen." *Journal of Marketing,* July 1977.

_____. "A Comparison of Japanese and U.S. Attitudes Towards Foreign Products." *Journal of Marketing,* Vol. 34, January 1970.

Nakanomyo, Takashi, "Distributors Use Information Management to Define Consumer Demands." *Business Japan,* October 1989.

"A Nation that Just Loves to Consume." *The Economist,* July 2, 1988.

"Obstacles to Exporting Faced by Small Business." Hearing before the Committee on Small Business, United States Senate, Ninety-Eighth Congress, 1st Session, February 11, 1983.

O'Neill, Robert, "Go West Young Man—To Japan?" *Progressive Grocer,* January 1984.

"The Opening of Japan." *The Economist,* December 17, 1988.

"Outline of Japanese Distribution Structures." The Distribution Economics Institute of Japan. Published by the Nihon Keizai Shimbum. 1973–74 Enlarged Edition.

Pucik, Vladimir, "Joint Ventures with the Japanese, the Key Role of HRM. *Euro-Asia Business Review,* October 1987.

Rockwell, Keith M., "Japanese Land Use, Business Practices Hurt Some U.S. Firms." *The Journal of Commerce,* December 20, 1989.

_____. "Playing by Japan's Rules Pays Off: Anheuser-Busch Finds Success." *The Journal of Commerce,* December 20, 1989.

Ross, Randolph E., "Understanding the Japanese Distribution System: An Explanatory Framework." *European Journal of Marketing,* Vol. 17, No. 1, 1983.

Sanekata, Kenji, "Antitrust in Japan: Recent Trends and Their Socio-Political Backgrounds." *University of British Columbia Law Review,* Vol. 20, No. 2, 1986.

_____. "Sole Import Agents: More Harm than Good?" *Economic Eye,* Summer 1990.

Sasaki, Mitsuo, "*TATENE*: A Vertical Restraint on Prices in Distribution." *The Yachiyo Journal of International Studies,* Vol. III, No. 1, April 1990.

Schlesinger, Jacob M., "U.S., Japan Make Progress in SII Talks, Say Final Pact May Be Reached Today." *The Wall Street Journal,* June 28, 1990.

"Seibu Considering Flexible Job Program." *Japan Times,* March 10, 1984.

The Seibu Group, 1984 Annual Report. Tokyo, 1984.

Shimaguchi, Mitsuaki and Larry J. Rosenberg, "Demystifying Japanese Distribution." *Columbia Journal of World Business,* Spring 1979.

Shiotani, Takahide, "Outline of Japanese Distribution System." *Business Japan,* August 1988.

Shioya, Takafusa, "Japan's Distribution System Is a Result of Economy, Society and Culture—MITI." *Business Japan,* August 1989.

"Strategies for Alleviating Recurrent Bilateral Trade Problems Between Japan and the United States." *The Japanese Non-Tariff Trade Barrier Issue: American Views and Implications for Japan—U.S. Trade Relations.* Report to the Japanese National Institute for Research Advancement. Arthur D. Little, Inc. May 1979.

"Structural Stuttering." *The Economist,* September 9, 1989.

Tabner, Jody, "Lagging Recovery in Japan Adds to Record U.S. Deficit." *Business America,* Vol. 6, No. 17, August 22, 1983.

Takahashi, Keiji, "Consumer Lobby Lacking." *Journal of Japanese Trade and Industry,* No. 3, 1990.

"Today's Challenge to American Business School Education." Business Schools' Deans Conference, The White House. The United States Department of Commerce and U.S.–Japan Communication. 1983.

"Too Many Shopkeepers." *The Economist,* January 28, 1989.

Troiano, Peter, "Trade Talk: Now in its 26th year, the Japan–U.S. Business Conference Gathers Experts to Tackle Bilateral Problems." *Economic World,* September 1989.

Tsuji, Yoshihiko. "Regulation of Resale Price Maintenance in Japan." *New York Law Forum,* Vol. 18, No. 2, 1972.

Tsurumi, Yoshi. "From Brinksmanship to Statesmanship: Refuting America's Attempts to 'Contain' Japan." *Pacific Basin Quarterly,* No. 16, Winter/Spring 1990.

_____. "Managing Consumer and Industrial Systems in Japan." *Sloan Management Review,* Fall 1982.

"The United Kingdom Market for Machine Tools." Prepared for the Japan Trade Center. London, December 1983.

"U.S.-Japan Distribution Discord." *Tokyo Business Today,* November 1988.

"U.S., Japan, Europe Sign Agreement of Patent Cooperation." *Business America,* October 31, 1983.

United States Congress, "Hearings before the Committee on Foreign Affairs, House of Representatives." Washington, D.C.: U.S. Government Printing Office, March-August 1982.

United States International Trade Commission. *Japan's Distribution System and Options for Improving U.S. Access.* Washington, D.C., June 1990.

Valéry, Nicholas, "Crunch in the Ginza-dori." *BZW Pacific,* February 1989.

Wallace, Cynthia Day, "Foreign Direct Investment: The Japan Dividend." Washington, D.C.: Center for Strategic and International Studies, 1990.

Weigand, Robert E., "The Gray Market Comes to Japan." *Columbia Journal of World Business.* Fall 1989.

Weil, Frank A. and Norman D. Glick, "Japan—Is the Market Open?" *Law and Policy in International Business.* Vol. 11, No. 3, 1979.

Willoughby, David G., "Adapting Successfully to the Japanese Market." *Journal of the ACCJ.* June 1981.

Yoffie, David B., and Milner, Helen V., "An Alternative to Free Trade or Protectionism: Why Corporations Seek Strategic Trade Policy." *California Management Review.* Summer 1989.

Japanese Government Publications: JETRO and MITI Materials

JETRO Publications

"Comparison Between the United Kingdom and Japan on the Distribution of Machine Tools and Suggestions." Overseas Economic Information Center.

"Doing Business in Japan." Marketing Series 8, Tokyo, revised 1982.

"Establishment of a Representative Office in Japan." *A Guide for Foreign Businessmen,* 1989.

"Foreign Companies in Japan." *Now in Japan,* No. 33, 1982.

Ichihashi, Tatsuhiko. "Hang In There! How to Sell in the Japanese Market." Delivered at the JETRO Business Round Table Meeting, Tokyo, September 21, 1982. *Speaking of Japan,* March 1983.

"Improvements of Japan's Standards and Certification Systems." Special Report, July 1983.

"Inside the Japanese Market for Manufactured Imports." Tokyo, 1983.

"Japan as an Export Market." Marketing Series 1, Tokyo, revised 1983.

"The Japanese Consumer." Marketing Series 6, Tokyo, revised 1983.

"Japanese Market-Opening and Import Promotion Measures." Information File 4, February 1984.

"Japan's Import and Marketing Regulations—Selected Consumer Products." Marketing Series 11, Tokyo, revised 1980.

"Market for Machine Tools in Japan." Overseas Economic Information Center, January 1984.

"Marketing and Distribution Strategies of Foreign Products in Japan." Tokyo, undated.

"Passenger Automobile Market in Japan." Overseas Economic Information Center, January 1984.

"Planning for Distribution in Japan." Marketing Series 5, Tokyo, revised 1980.

"Sales Promotion in the Japanese Market." Marketing Series 7, Tokyo, revised 1983.

"Setting Up a Business in Japan." *A Guide for Foreign Businessmen,* 1989.

"Sixth Workshop on Japan's Distribution Systems and Business Practices." Manufactured Imports Promotion Organization (MIPRO) & JETRO, October 27, 1989.

"Softnomics." Tokyo, 1984.

"The Japanese Distribution System," *JETRO MONITOR,* Vol. 5, No. 10, January 1991.

MITI Publications

An Analysis of and Recommendations Regarding the Japanese Distribution System and Business Practices. Manufactured Imports Promotion Committee, Tokyo, 1983.

"Asian-Pacific Cooperation and Its Future Direction." April 1989.

"The Distribution System In Japan." May 1989.

"The Distribution System In Japan." February 1990.

Gaishikei kigyo no doko (Trends in Foreign-Affiliated Companies). Tokyo, annual.

"Interim Report: Planning Subcommittee on Improving the Quality of Life, 1990's Policy Committee, Industrial Structural Council (Summary)." May 9, 1990.

"Import Expansion Measures." January 1990.

"Japan's Responsibilities and Initiatives Approaching the New Century—Aimed at Formulating Multilayered International Relations." May 1990.

"Japan's Trade—Recent Trends." January 1990.

"MITI's New External Policies for the 1990s." January 1990.

"The Nineteenth Survey on Japanese Business Activities Abroad." March 1990.

"Penetrating the Japanese Market." Committee for Manufactured Goods Import Measures, Manufactured Imports Promotion Organization, No. 3, July 1980.

"The Performance of Foreign-Affiliated Companies." Annual.

Selling Japan from A to Z. Edited by the Ministry of International Trade and Industry, Tokyo.

"Summary of MITI's Vision for the Distribution System in the 1990s." Tokyo, September 1989.

"The Twenty-third Survey on Business Activities of Foreign Affiliates in Japan." March 1990.

"U.S.-Japan Trade Today—Must We Not Come to Realize 'the Other Facts'?" April 1990.

"White Paper on Economic Cooperation 1988 (Summary)." Tokyo, August 1989.

"White Paper on International Trade, 1983." Tokyo, 1983.

Index

A

Abegglen, James C., 2
Acquisitions, 167-70
Action program, 21
Adanac Trading Company, 125
Africa, 10
Aichi, 89, 101
Airbus Industries, 150
Aizu-Toko, 169
Ajinomoto, 158
Allied Import Co., 104
Allied-Lyons, 158
Allstate Life Insurance, 158
ALS, 169
America, 158
American, 175
   semiconductors, 22
   Congressmen, 22
   Chamber of Commerce, 144
   Chamber of Commerce in Japan, 61
   companies, 21
   contractors, 22
Amsterdam diamond district, 87
Amway, 152
Angora wool, 178

Anheuser-Busch, 179
Antimonopoly Act, 40, 66
Antitrust rules, 65
Apple Computers, 152, 163
Asahi Beer, 44
Asahi Chemical, 158
Asahi Glass, 151
Asahi Medical, 169
Automotive industry, 13

B

Banks, 66
   Dai-Ichi Kangyo Bank (DKB), 33, 40
   Fuji Bank, 40
   Industrial Bank of Japan (IBJ), 33, 40
   Sanwa Bank, 40, 43
   Sumitomo Bank, 33, 39, 40, 43, 70,
      148, 158
   Tokai Bank, 40, 43, 51
Banyu, 169
BASF, 70, 163
Baskin-Robbins, 151, 152
Bayer Yakuhin 158, 170
Bayer, 70, 163
Beiersdorf, 145

Bendix Japan, 174
Berry Brothers & Rudd, 145
Bloomingdale's, 125
BMW, 2, 145, 152, 163, 164
Boards of Directors, 42
Bonus program, 106
Borden, 158
Braun, 144, 145
Brinton, 150
Bristol Meyers, 164
Bristol-Meyers Lion, 158
British Museum, 125
Bureaucratic intervention, 15

C
C. Itoh, 43, 148, 150
Caldbeck-MacGregor, 150
Campbell Soup, 163, 170
Canadian Dream Mail-Order Magazine, 125
Canon, 152
Capital goods, 11
Caterpillar, 158
CBS, 158, 167
Census of Commerce, 91 103
Chain store, *see* Retailer chain store
Chanel, 152
Channels 1990, 81
Channel geometry, 83
Channel members, 92, 174, 179
Channel system, 85
Channel system; multilayered, 82
Channel commitment, 84
Chiba, 89, 101
Christie's, 151
Ciba-Geigy, 164
Citibank, 144
Closed market, 4
Coca Cola, 2, 144, 145, 163
Commercial Activities Adjustments
    Boards, 119
Commercial Census, 118
Computerization, 66
Consumer,
    attitude change, 132
    behavioral changes, 131

brand names, 131
convenience, 131
craft orientation, 132
cultural events focus, 132
cycle of preference, 136
demands, 84
fashion orientation, 132
financing, 132, 136
goods, 26, 57, 58, 76, 78, 103
income levels, 131
information, 135
leisure time, 132
needs diversified, 131
products, 76
self-service, 131
Consumer products, 103
Control, 58
Convenience stores, 100
Coopervision, 169
Corning, 151, 152, 157
Corning Glass Works, 169, 170
Corning Japan, 170
Corporate alignments, 31
Cosmetics Industry, 85
Credit cards, 136
Cross-holdings, 36, 40, 66, 168
Customs tariff rate, 13
Customs inspectors, 15

D
Daiei, 53, 59, 103
Daihatsu, 53
Danforth, Senator John, 22
Data General, 169
David's Cookies, 150
Debit cards, 136
Del Monte, 145
Denmark, 150
Department stores, 99, 100, 122
Discounts, 105
Digital Equipment Corporation, 4, 69
Direct marketing, 124
Directors, appointment, 59
Distribution system, 75, 81, 111, 184
    alternatives, 96
    decentralized, 84

features, 84
geographic limitations, 84
obstacle, 26
pay for service, 84
privacy laws, 136
report 1984, 26
retail, 35, 92
returns, 94
Dodwell, 47, 69, 150
Door-to-door, 122, 124
Dow Chemical, 158
DuPont, 157, 158, 163
Duskin, 151

E
Eastern Europe, 188
Eastman Kodak, 163, 169
Economic cooperation, 42
Economic Planning Agency, 26, 175
Electrolux, 152
Electronics, 10
Eli Lilly, 164
Emerson Electric, 169
EMI, 158
Endaka, 175, 176
Esso, 163
Europe, 10, 20, 26, 151, 165, 167, 175
European Business Community, 144
Everready (Union Carbide), 158
Exporters U.S., 81
Exports, 3, 9, 184
Exxon, 163

F
Fair Trade Commission (FTC), 38, 66,
    67, 187
Fair trade, 10
Family Mart, 151
Fauchon, 145
Fila, 145
Financing, 84
Firestone, 167
Ford, 150
Foreign,
    banks, 66
    businesses, 25

businessman, 4
companies, 10, 66, 69
Exchange Control Law, 20
films, 81
goods, 26
governments, 27, 66
pressure, 65
Fortune 500, 146
Franchise chains, 122
Franchising, 147, 149
Franklin Mint, 152
French, 68, 177
Fuji Tekko, 50
Fuji, 53, 158, 176
Fuji Heavy Industries, 48, 50
Fujisawa-Astra, 158
Fujita, 151 158
Fujiya, 151
Fukuoka, 89, 101
Funai, 169
Fuyo Group, 43, 51, 70

G
Gaiatsu, 65
General Foods, 158
General Electric, 163, 170
General Agreement on Tariffs and Trade
    (GATT), 19, 20, 22, 27
Germany, 3, 10, 68, 107, 125, 174, 178
Ginza, 176
Givaudan, 164
Glaxo, 164
Goodyear, 151
Government, 26
    agencies, 21
    Japanese, 65
    ministries, 21
    procurement, 21, 25, 26
    red tape, 26
Governments foreign, 65
Grace, Peter, 2
Grace Japan, 164
Great Britian, 3, 10
Greeley, Horace, 138
Groupings, 31, 35, 68, 69, 70
    bank loans, 36

banks, 40
barrier, 65
capital keiretsu, 32
common image, 37
distribution keiretsu, 32, 36, 40, 61, 75
employee relations, 37
enterprise keiretsu, 32, 47
exchange of personnel, 36
family, 51
industrial, 34
insurance companies, 43
joint-venture partner, 61
keiretsu joint ventures, 36
loyalty, 61
manufacturers, 53
Matsushita, 48, 49
members, 37
Mitsui, 41
Nippon Steel, 47
organization, 48
ryutsu keiretsu, 57
stock purchase, 36
structure, 36
Toshiba, 50
vertical, 33, 36, 47, 50, 62, 66
zaibatsu, 40
GTE, 158
Gucci, 2, 175

H
Hakuhodo, 158
Hakuraihin, 150
Henderson, Dan Fenno, 37
Hercules, 158
Hermes, 151, 175
Hewlett-Packard, 163
Hino, 50
Hiroshima, 89, 101
Hitachi, 33, 47, 48, 62, 176
Hokkaido 89, 101
Holding companies, 39
Honda, 33, 63
Honeywell-NEC, 158
Hong Kong, 144
Hoya, 59, 63
Hughes Aircraft, 150

Hyogo, 89, 101

I
IBM, 2, 144, 145, 163, 164, 165
ICI, 158
Ikebukuro shopping area, 176
Imports, 9, 78, 93
    board, 27
    costs, 103
    direct, 103
    distribution alternatives, 104
    duties, 103
    fairs, 27
    indirect, 103
    Italian Spaghetti, 104
    restrictions, 20
    targets, 27
    users, 150
    vs. export, 10
Industrial policy, 15, 21, 25, 121
Industrial Policy Bureau, Ministry of
    Trade and Industry, 111
Inefficiencies, 81
Information flow, 135
Information revolution, 185
Innovations and changes, 76
Intel, 163
Intercompany links, 68
Intermediaries, 82
Intermediate goods, 11
International Monetary Fund (IMF), 19
International Trade Commission, 81, 146
Inventory, 84
Investment, 16
Ishihara, 179
Ishikawajima-Harima Heavy Industries
    (IHI), 50
Italians, 68
Ito Yokado, 53, 59, 103, 123, 152
Iwaki Glass, 152, 157
Izumiya, 119

J
Japan,
    External Trade Organization (JETRO),
        27, 187

Federation of Economic Organizations (Keidanren), 26, 68
Statistical Yearbook: 1989, 101
Japanese National Railways, 16, 21
Jardine, 150
Johnson & Johnson, 145, 146, 163, 178
Joint ventures, 155-7
Jusco, 53, 104
Just in time (JIT), 179

K
K. Hattori, 59, 158
Kanagawa, 89, 101
Kanematsu-Gosho, 43, 148
Karl Zeiss, 145
Kasuda Business Machines, 169
Kato, Makoto, 163, 164
Keidanren, 26, 28
Keiretsu, 4, 26, 27, 31, 33, 35, 36, 37, 42, 57, 59, 65, 66, 67, 68, 70, 75, 113, 148, 149, 168, 184, 187
    capital, 39
    distribution, 37, 38, 61, 62, 63, 67
    horizontal 37, 38, 39
    kigyo, 48
    production, 47
Kennedy Round, 19
Kentucky Fried Chicken, 150, 151, 158
Kimberly Clark, 158
Kirin, 158
Kodak, 145
Koito, 169
Komatsu, 158
Konaga, Keiichi, 111
Korea, 69, 151
Kyoritsu, 169
Kyoto, 89, 101, 119

L
L.L.Bean, 125
Large Store Law, 117
Latin America, 10
Lego, 145, 163, 164
Levis, 145, 164
Liberal Democratic Party, 20, 68
Licensing, 147, 149

Lifetime employment, 157, 168
Limitations of retail, 84
Lipton, 145
Louis Vuitton, 145
Loyalty, 35
Lux, 145

M
Mail order, 124
Mailing lists, 126
Malcolm Baldrige National Quality Award, 175
Management and Coordination Agency, 89
Market entry,
    alternatives, 150
    breakup problems, 157
    commitment, 143
    consulting firms, 143
    distribution access, 155
    distribution channels, 157
    exporting, 147, 148, 156
    failure rate, 146
    financial burden, 156
    franchising, 147, 149
    hostile takeover, 169
    importer, 141, 149
    intermediaries, 147, 148
    licensing, 147, 149
    local partner, 156
    opening packages, 21
    partner, 141, 142, 143, 144
    partner size, 156
    pricing difficulty, 150
    product factors, 142
    successes and failures, 144
    theoretical considerations, 147, 155
    wholly-owned cost factors, 161
    wholly-owned strategic product, 163
    wholly-owned personnel, 162
Marketing channels, 62
Mars, 151
Marubeni, 43, 148
Matsushita, 33, 47, 48, 50, 53, 59, 62, 63, 70, 176
Matsushita Electric Trading, 50
Matsuzakaya, 125, 126

Max Factor, 165
Maxwell House Coffee, 158
Mazda, 44
McCann-Erickson, 158
McDonald's, 2, 144, 151, 158
McGraw-Hill, 158
Meiji, 158
Melita, 145
Mercedes Benz, 152, 163
Merck, 163, 169
Merrel Dow, 169
Miles-Sankyo, 158
Mining, 44
Ministry of Agriculture, 15
Ministry of Finance, 67, 144
Ministry of Health, 15
Ministry of Home Affairs, 121
Ministry of International Trade and Indus-
    try (MITI), 10, 15, 67, 91, 103, 118,
    119, 15, 21, 22, 27, 119, 121, 123,
    125, 126, 135, 144
3M, 158
MIPRO, 187
Mitsubishi, 33, 39, 40, 43, 63, 148, 150,
    151, 158
Mitsui, 33, 39, 40, 43, 51, 148, 150, 157
Mitsui & Co., 43
Mitsukoshi, 151
Mobil, 163
Moore, 158
Morita, Akio, 179
MOSS (market-oriented sector specific),
    21
Motorola, 163, 164, 169
Movement of goods, 84
Mr. Donut, 151, 152
MTS, 153
Musashino, 158
Mutual adjustments,
    centralized distribution, 184
    change, 183
    close market contact, 186
    delivery, 179
    expected perfection, 174
    firms outside Japan, 184, 185
    further market openings, 184

international competitiveness, 185
keihakutansho, 177
lack of quality, 173, 174
long-term perspective, 179
managerial time, 186
market importance, 184
private sector, 184
public relations tactics, 188
quality control, 174, 175, 185
trading partner policies, 189
understand constraints, 184
value, 177

N
Nagoya, 125
Nakasone, Prime Minister, 21, 27
Nasco, 170
Nationalism, 31
Nescafe, 2
Nestle, 144, 145, 163, 164
Network retail, 62
Network wholesale, 62
Network integrated marketing, 57
New product introduction, 93
New products, 92, 93
New technology, 137
New York, 176
Newly industrialized countries (NICs), 176
Nichimen, 43, 148, 150
Nikkei, 158
Nippon Steel, 32, 33, 47
Nippon Gakki, 59
Nippon Mini-Computer, 169
Nippon Telegraph and Telephone, 16, 21
Nippondenso, 50
Nissan, 33, 47, 48, 50, 53, 59, 63
Nissan Group, 51, 52
Nissho Iwai, 43, 148, 150
Non-tariff barriers (NTBs), 20, 75

O
Office of the Trade Ombudsman, 21
Oil crises 1973, 1979, 9
Okamoto Industries, 158
Olivetti, 145
Open market, 3, 4, 65, 67

Organization for Economic Cooperation
    and Development, 19, 20
Osaka, 88, 89, 100, 101
OSRAM Ltd., 151, 174

P
Pampers, 145
Parent companies, 36
Personnel transfer, 50, 58
Pfizer, 163, 170
Philip Morris, 150
Philips, 70, 163
Philips Petroleum, 158
Pickens, Boone, 169
Pitney-Bowes, 151
Point of sale (POS), 136
Polaroid, 145, 163
Population, 1
POS scanners, 136, 137
Prewar period, 42, 57
Prewar economic development, 39
Price importance, 175
Price survey 1990, 175, 176
Proctor & Gamble, 146
Product alterations, 177, 178
Product holism, 177
Production system development, 82
Protectionism, 10, 190
Puma, 145

Q
Quality control, 174, 175, 185
Quotas, 3

R
R.J.Reynolds, 150
Ralph Lauren, 151
Ralston Purina, 158
Recruitment problem, 157
Reebok, 158
Reilly, Edmund J., 4, 69
Reliability and service, 178, 179, 185
Remy Martin, 145
Research and development, 21
Retail distribution, 26
Retailer,

application process, 120
area of concentration, 100
changes in sales, 122
channel member support, 107
convenience, 122
decline, 107
demanding consumers, 106
department stores, 99, 100, 122
Department Store Law, 118, 119
direct imports 1988, 121
disadvantages 1985, 88
electric appliance, 122
establishments, 100, 101
financing, 105, 107
food supermarkets, 122
general merchandise, 100, 122
gift packaging, 107
growth, 117
import efficiency, 121
imports increase, 151
integrated selling, 106
integration, 66
lack of openings, 120
Large-Scale Retail Store Law, 117,
    119, 120
local area councils, 119
local government, 120
location, 99
long-term commitment, 107
mail-order, 122
market research, 107
marketers of culture, 131
new structure emergence, 121
presentation, 106
process, 105
purchasing clubs, 106
purchasing costs, 121
restricted establishment, 119
returns, 105
sales, 91
service, 105, 106, 107
service orientation, 107
size, 101, 103, 117
soft research, 107
specialty stores, 100
structural changes, 117

structure, 99
tracking consumer taste, 106
trends, 118
Retailer chain store,
   centralized purchasing, 124
   development, 123
   Family Mart, 124
   franchise, 123
   information system, 124
   Kei Mart, 124
   Lawson, 124
   locations, 123
   management, 123
   My Shop, 124
   planned increase 1991, 123
   Sun Chin, 124
   Sunshop, 124
   volume, 123,
   voluntary chains, 122
   Yamazaki, 124
Retailer, non-store,
   Amway, 124
   cable television, 126
   Franklin Mint, 125
   Fuji Television Network, 126
   Fujisankei Living Service, 126
   HI-OVIS, 126
   mail products, 125
   mailing costs, 126
   party approach, 124
   Quelle, 125, 126
   Shaklee, 124
   Tupperware, 124
   World Shopping System Network, 127
   Yunyua, 125
Retirement, 84
Return policy, 94, 105
RJR Nabisco, 158
Robotization, 66
Rorer Group, 169
Rosenthal, 107
Royal Doulton, 151
Royal Institute of International Studies, 3

S
Saitama, 89, 101

Salomon S.A., 177
Salomon Sports, 152
Samsung, 151
Sandoz, 163
Sanyo, 62
Schering-Plough, 163
Schick, 144, 154, 158
Science and Technology Agency, 15
Seagram, 158
Searle Yakuhin, 158
Sears, 121, 125, 152
Seibu Retail Group, 48, 50, 53, 59, 60,
   125, 132, 137, 151, 158
Seiko, 59, 63, 158
Seiyu store, 137, 138
Senmon shosha, 148
7-Eleven, 123, 124, 152, 158
Shaklee, 124, 158
Sharing responsibility, 84
Sharp, 63, 152
Sharper Image, 152
Sheplers, 125
Shipbuilding, 10
Shiseido, 58
Shizuoka, 89, 101, 119
Shopping centers, 122
Siemens, 151, 174
Smaller companies, 70
Social function fulfillment, 84
Sogo Shosha, 44, 50, 59, 66, 68, 77, 89,
   147, 148, 149, 150
Sony, 33, 63, 152, 158, 176
Southeast Asia, 151
Spaulding Japan, 177
Spirax Sarco Ltd., 151, 178
Squibb, 164
Stability, 35
Stalk, Jr., George, 2
Standards, 14
   bona fide, 14
   certificates of approval, 14
   modified, 14
Statistics Bureau, Management and Coor-
   dination Agency, 101
Steady supply, 84
Steel, 10

Storage, 94
Structural Impediments Initiative (SII), 27, 65, 120
Subaru, 50
Subcontracting, 51
Subsidiaries, 58
Suntory, 59, 158, 179
Super 301, 22, 27
Supplier network, 51
Support staff, 93
Suzuki, 63
Sweden, 152

T
Taiwan, 176
Taiyo Fishery, 158
Takeda, 169, 170
Tariffs, 3
Teijin, 151
Tetra Pak, 163
Texas Instruments, 163, 164
Textiles, 10
Tiffany, 125
Tobacco Monopoly, 16, 21
Toho, 169
Tokina, 170
Tokyo, 88, 89, 100, 101, 121, 125, 137, 151, 176
Tokyu, 48, 50, 53, 59
Tonya, 81
Toppan, 158
Toray, 157
Torii, 169
Toshiba, 48, 62, 158
Tower Records, 153
Toyo Keizai, 32, 69
Toyo Menka, 43, 148
Toyoda Loom, 50
Toyota, 33, 47, 48, 50, 53, 59, 63, 151, 174, 177
Toys R Us, 121, 152, 158
Trade,
   Act 1988, 27
   barriers, 4, 10, 13, 22, 25, 27
   buy foreign programs, 27
   closed market, 11

complaints, 21
conflicts, 9, 19
deficit, 10, 189
distribution system, 27
expansion, 9
exports, 10, 19, 22
fair trade, 22
forecasts, 22
imbalances, 10, 22
impediments, 13, 25
imports, 10
import fairs, 27
import restrictions, 13, 20
Import-buying missions, 27
incentives, 15
liberalization, 22
market opening, 25
negotiations, 4, 19, 20
Nontariff barriers (NTBs), 14, 15, 20, 25, 26
protection, 11, 19
quotas, 13, 14, 15, 20, 22, 25, 26
reciprocity, 22
rejected goods, 15
restrictions, 20, 188
statistics, 10
surplus, 9, 10
tariffs, 13, 14, 15, 25, 26
Western free traders, 22
Trading companies, 63, 66, 141, *see also* sogo shosha, senmon shosha
TRW, 163, 170
Tupperware, 124, 152
Twinings, 145

U
U.S. Japan Trade Study Group, 20
U.S. Department of Commerce, 26, 91
U.S. International Trade Commission (USITC), 81, 146
U.S. Advisory Committee for Trade Policy and Negotiations (ACTPN), 75
Ueshima Seisakusho, 169
United States, 3, 4, 10, 20, 22, 26, 35, 88, 89, 100, 101, 105, 107, 124, 126,

136, 141, 144, 165, 167, 175, 177, 189, 190
Upjohn, 164

V
Victor Harris, 165
Volvo, 151

W
W.R. Grace, 2
Warehouse efficiency, 114
Warner Lambert, 158
Waterford, 152
Wedgwood, 152
Wella, 145
Whirlpool, 152
Wholesale, 35
Wholesaler ties, 92
Wholesaler rebates, 95
Wholesalers, 58, 59, 63, 82, 84, 87, 88, 89, 91, 185
  advantages, 88
  cash-and-carry, 115
  changes since 1970, 112
  channel integration, 113
  channel research tool, 97
  competitiveness focus, 115
  consolidation, 114
  consumer migration, 114
  cost reduction, 95
  credit and financing, 97
  distribution channels, 112
  distribution improvements, 114
  distribution zones, 114
  financing, 114
  flexibility and accommodation of re-
    tailer, 97
  function, 87
  integration, 115
  keiretsu fashion, 113
  large, 89
  manufacturer to retailer, 114
  manufacturer-wholesalers, 113
  new distribution centers, 114
  new business relations, 115
  power as channel members, 112

  rapid delivery, good supply, 97
  regional, 114
  reorientation, 116
  sales, 91
  service support, 97
  sharing of risk, 97
  small, 89, 115, 117
  social ties, 97
  specialization, 114
  structural changes, 111, 112, 115
  transportation structure, 114
  trend since mid-80s, 112
World War II, 19

X
Xerox, 144, 158

Y
Yamaha, 63
Yamaichi Securities, 170
Yamazaki Bakery, 158
Yanase, 150, 151
Yen, 1, 20, 175
Yokado, 119
Yokogawa Electric, 170
Yokogawa-Hewlett-Packard, 158
Yoshida, Matt, 174
Yoshitomi Pharmaceutical, 170

Z
Zaibatsu, 39, 42
Zimmerman, Mark, 61, 68